A life tog

A LIFE TOGETHER

*The distribution of attitudes
around the disabled*

TIM DARTINGTON, ERIC MILLER,
and GERALDINE GWYNNE

TAVISTOCK PUBLICATIONS
LONDON AND NEW YORK

First published in 1981 by
Tavistock Publications Ltd
11 New Fetter Lane, London EC4P 4EE
Published in the USA by
Tavistock Publications
in association with Methuen, Inc.
733 Third Avenue, New York, NY 10017
© 1981 Crown copyright
Printed in Great Britain by
Richard Clay & Co,
Bungay, Suffolk

British Library Cataloguing in Publication Data

Dartington, T.
A life together: the distribution of attitudes
around the disabled
1. Physically handicapped - Great Britain
I. Title   II. Miller, E. J.
III. Gwynne, G. V.
362.4'0941   HV3024.G7A3

ISBN 0-422-77990-8
ISBN 0-422-77910-5 Pbk

Contents

Acknowledgements

In the nature of our study, the research team were working with many individuals and groups, whose willingness to explore ideas and experience with us has made possible the difficult task of looking anew at the thorny old problem of 'attitudes'.

Most must remain anonymous for reasons of confidentiality, but we can mention the following participants in a workshop at the King's Fund Centre: Stephen Bradshaw (Spinal Injuries Association); J. A. Bromage (Manpower Services Commission); Joan Butterworth (Milton Keynes Development Corporation); Hazel Canter, Dr Doreen Rothman (DHSS); Peter Cobb (London Borough of Newham); Jerry Conway, Jack Hughes (London Borough of Camden); Mary Froud (Newham Association for the Disabled); Susy Large, Peter Large (Association of Disabled Professionals); Jean Potterton, Michael Stopford (Spastics Society); Joan Thompson (disabled resident, London Borough of Camden); Linda Tuckey (researcher, Leicestershire); Peter Barham, Michael Norris (Tavistock Institute); Diana Irish, David Towell (King's Fund Centre).

We would emphasize that this was not research done *on* individuals, or the groups and organizations they represent. Rather we were asking if they would work with us in examining ways in which they – and everybody else – express different attitudes in their interactions as disabled people or as those living or working with disabled people. We would like to record here our appreciation of the help we were given.

In two cases we were able to observe changes in practice in the care of disabled people. These examples were of the greatest help in looking at shifts of emphasis in the distribution of attitudes. In the circumstances it is not appropriate to maintain their anonymity, so special thanks go to the co-ordinating committee of The Spastics Society and the first residents who participated in their residential care scheme in

Acknowledgements

Milton Keynes, and to the staff and residents of the new residential unit in the London Borough of Camden.

Finally we would like to thank the Department of Health and Social Security, for funding most of the costs of this exploratory project.

1
Approaching the study of attitudes

HAS ANYTHING REALLY CHANGED?

Campaigns against prejudice and discrimination will probably be remarked on by future social historians as a feature of
the 1960s and 1970s. Assumptions and values that had seemed
serviceable for many years, and even generations, have been
subjected to rigorous criticism and challenge. Indeed, 1968
may well be remembered as being just as pivotal as 1848 was
for nineteenth-century Europe.

The campaigns can chalk up significant successes. In the
case of racial discrimination, the black movement in the
United States led the way in a two-pronged approach, which
on the one side used the legislative machinery to secure and
enforce equal rights, and on the other side began to provide
blacks with an alternative identity with its own historical roots
(the need for which Arthur Haley resonated so successfully):
black became beautiful. Britain produced its legislation, with
the Commission on Racial Equality as its watchdog. The path
has not been an easy one, and we are reminded of this by a riot
in Bristol or a National Front demonstration. Nevertheless,
there is an air of greater tolerance, or at least an increasing
acceptance that the society we are living in is multi-racial. The
campaign for women's rights has had similar outcomes.
Despite the chequered progress of the Equal Opportunities
Commission, it is evident that time-honoured assumptions
about sexual roles are increasingly being undermined – and
not only among middle-class intellectuals. A third movement,
Gay Liberation, has yet to acquire its statutory watchdog, but
prejudice against homosexuals shows signs of beginning to be
eroded.

However, it has to be noted that alongside the liberalization
in the attitudes of whites toward blacks, men towards women,
heterosexuals towards homosexuals – and we use the word
'alongside' because cause and consequence are difficult to

1

separate – there has also been the emergence of more extreme groupings amongst the disadvantaged categories: for example, Black Muslims, Rastafarians, radical anti-male women's groups, and so on. Tacitly, if not explicitly, they are saying to the rest of the society that the tolerance, the acceptance, the removal of discriminatory practices are suspect – placatory, even token, shifts in attitudes designed to keep power in the same hands as before. Acceptance and integration are threats to an identity that is based on difference and separation: hence the difference has to be asserted in ways that are more extreme, more violent, and sometimes seemingly irrational and bizarre. So to women all men are rapists; to blacks all police are the enemy – agents of the white society.

We make this point because the interconnectedness of attitudes has been a central theme throughout our study, and the kinds of processes we have just outlined are not without parallels in the world of disability. Disabled people too seem to be 'coming out'. As with race and gender, the movement towards change had been gathering momentum during the 1950s. When the Royal Commission on the Law relating to Mental Illness and Mental Deficiency reported in 1957, it recommended a shift in emphasis from custodial care in the large, antique hospitals towards community-based care. (In the United States, the recommendations of a corresponding Joint Commission in 1960 were almost identical.) The consequent Mental Health Act of 1959 produced a great exodus of patients from hospitals but little in the way of community resources to cope with them. Not until the Health and Public Services Act of 1968 were local authorities statutorily obliged to provide residential care. In the case of the physically handicapped and chronic sick, there was no direct equivalent of the 1959 Act. However, the burgeoning during the 1950s of voluntary homes for such people – the Cheshire Homes being a well-known example – reflected a similar reaction against custodial hospital care, though the emphasis may have been slightly different. For the mentally ill and handicapped it was being postulated that institutionalization was an impediment to treatment and rehabilitation and hence much hope was invested in the therapeutic potential of hostels, half-way houses, and other forms of community care. For the physically handicapped and chronic sick there was less investment in hopes of rehabilitation – though these were not absent – but it was argued forcefully that young people who were mentally alert, even though physically incurable, should not be condemned to spend the rest of their lives among senile and demented patients in geriatric wards.

Escape from hospitals into residential homes was such a relief for most inmates that they were far more grateful for the new opportunities than critical of constraints. This was to change. In an earlier book we described the emergence, during the late 1950s and early 1960s, of demands by the residents of one Cheshire Home for more self-determination (Miller and Gwynne 1972, Chapter 2). They were predominantly concerned with having a greater say in managing their own lives in their own institution. But also gaining ground was a more widespread notion of unjust discrimination against the disabled and the beginnings of a movement akin to the campaigns against racial and sexual discrimination. The disabled and their able-bodied advocates were protesting at the social and economic handicaps that went along with physical disabilities: equality of treatment, or positive discrimination, was becoming defined not so much as a privilege but as a legitimate right. And, alongside this political activity, was an emerging 'disabled consciousness' movement akin, for example, to black consciousness in the United States. This was evidenced in 1966 with the formation of the Disablement Income Group to campaign for a disability pension to be payable as a matter of right and to be based on the degree rather than on the causes of disablement. Its founder, the late Megan du Boisson, was herself restricted to a wheelchair by multiple sclerosis, and the rapidity with which local DIG branches formed all over Britain suggested that her initiative was something that a lot of people had been waiting for. The same year saw publication of a book of papers by disabled people edited by the late Paul Hunt (Hunt 1966). Many of the writers were still looking upon themselves as deviants in the normal world – this was the reality to which they had somehow to adapt and adjust – but a few, including Hunt himself, were beginning to take a more radical stance: they insisted on being perceived as *part* of the normal world, to which they had a distinctive contribution to

3

make. Hunt's perspective at that time was primarily philosophical – he was arguing lucidly that the experience of disability added an extra dimension to our understanding of the relationship of the individual to society – but later he was to take up an explicitly political position: that it is society which handicaps the disabled. The Union of the Physically Impaired, of which he was a founder, was much closer in ideology to the 'black power' movement in asserting that only the disabled could understand the needs of the disabled and that only through the struggle of the disabled themselves could the requisite changes in society be achieved: they rejected able-bodied spokesmen for their cause.

During the late 1960s and 1970s the able-bodied advocates were nevertheless active. In Parliament, a private member was piloting the Chronically Sick and Disabled Persons Bill. Backed by the government of the day, it became law in 1970, and the private member concerned, Alf Morris, was to become the first incumbent of a new position as Minister for the Disabled, with a mandate to protect and advance the position of the disabled not only from within the Department of Health and Social Security, where he was based, but in relation to the activities of other government departments too. The aim of the 1970 Act was to get rid of various forms of discrimination and to provide means through which people with disabilities could be helped to participate in society to the fullest possible extent. It obliged local authorities first to identify all the disabled in their areas and second to make sure that they had the necessary equipment and adaptations in their homes, and also access to entertainment and other amenities outside.

The Act was passed at a time when the major reorganization of the National Health Service was being discussed and debated. The first Green Paper had been issued by the Ministry of Health in 1970. Like many others we were hopeful that the reorganization (which eventually came in 1974) would have positive consequences, building on the 1970 Act:

'An area organization in which the boundaries of health authorities and local authorities coincide should have many advantages. In particular, it should become more possible to design and implement strategies of domiciliary and community care on the one hand and the use of residential institutions on the other.'   (Miller and Gwynne 1972:222)

These hopes have been largely unfulfilled. In the case of mental illness the effect of the 1959 Mental Health Act in Britain and its equivalent in the USA has been recently summed up as follows:

'The stage was set both in the UK and the States for a major reorientation in mental health care; the reality has been a major reduction in the mental hospital population, unaccompanied by a corresponding increase in community resources.'   (Jansen 1980: 16)

For the physically handicapped the story is much the same. In terms of community care and services, the performance of many local authorities has been lamentable.[1] Integration of local authority and health service provision has at best been patchy and was not helped by the NHS's ill-advised investment in a larger number of specialized hospital units for the younger chronic sick and physically handicapped. In terms of economic discrimination, the only significant gain has been the mobility allowance. The idea of the disability pension, which could provide at least a semblance of independence, choice, and self-respect, seems as far from realization as ever.

Both despite and because of these failures, the position of the physically disabled population nevertheless appears to have shifted. Following the 1970 Act, accessibility for example has been taken more seriously. The wheelchair symbol, though far from ubiquitous, has become much more widespread, and wheelchair users themselves are thus to be seen more often than before in shops and other public places. Failures have meant that the cause of the disabled has been taken up more vigorously, more visibly, and by more bodies. For example, the Disability Alliance 'was set up in 1974 in response to the disappointing proposals contained in the White Paper "Social Security Provision for Chronically Sick and Disabled People"

[1]In 1977–78 . . . the London Borough of Newham helped 8.9 per 1000 of its population with adaptations to their houses, and Solihull virtually no one; Islington helped 18.3 per 1000 with telephones, Cambridgeshire 0.1' (Ann Shearer, *The Guardian*, 21 May 1980).

5

(July 1974)', and is now a federation of over sixty organizations for and of disabled people.

> 'In the words of one of its members, the founding organizations were "united in fury" at the failure to introduce an allowance paid as of right to all disabled people, and that the Government's proposals would create new anomalies, and so further delay a comprehensive approach to financial provision for disability.'   (The Disability Alliance 1980)

Well over 300 organizations of and for disabled people are listed at the end of the Alliance's annual Disability Rights Handbook. At the Establishment end of the spectrum, the two longstanding Royal National Institutes, for the Blind and for the Deaf, have been joined by another 'Royal': the Central Council for the Disabled and the British Association for Rehabilitation of the Disabled have merged into RADAR, the Royal Association for Disability and Rehabilitation. At the other end are more radical and activist groups which, like the Union of the Physically Impaired, are led and run by the disabled themselves: thus NUD – the National Union of the Deaf – is the grassroots counterpart of RNID.

With this heightened activity, the special needs of people working with the handicapped have received greater attention. The Williams Committee, on the staffing of residential homes in general, had reported in 1967 (National Council of Social Service 1967). The Open University course *The Handicapped Person in the Community* has attracted several thousand students since it was launched in 1975. Media coverage has also greatly[1] increased. There has been a succession of regular television and radio programmes for and about the disabled: for example, *Does He Take Sugar?* and the Sunday morning *Link* series. (ATV Network Limited is a co-publisher of the Disability Rights Handbook.) The Crossroads care attendant scheme was a direct if unplanned product of the television programme. There has also been a number of one-off documentaries and dramas. In 1979–80 the London stage has offered *Whose Life Is It Anyway?* and *Duet for One*, both about people with incurable illnesses, together with *Wings* (a stroke victim), *The Elephant Man* (the problems of hideous deformity) – back in London after a highly successful run in New York –

and, on the theme of the elderly in institutions, *The Gin Game*, originating from the United States. New York playgoers are also currently (July 1980) being shown *Children of a Lesser God*, featuring a totally deaf young woman. 1981, designated as the International Year of Disabled People, is intended to intensify this process: more campaigns, more television documentaries, more dramas to attract public attention. The National Film Theatre arranged a season of films on the theme 'Carry on, Cripple'.

The campaigning, ferment, and publicity over these twenty years must surely have had a significant effect on public prejudices and attitudes. Or have they? Has racism been reduced or simply disappeared underground? The social fact is that black youths still have a lower chance of getting a job than any other group. Sexual discrimination is still widely practised and the *Guardian* has no difficulty in filling its weekly column, 'The Naked Ape', with examples of sexism. Or perhaps, as we suggested earlier, the association of greater understanding and tolerance on the one side with more assertive and extremist positions on the other has meant that the gap and the conflict seem as intractable as before? As for physical handicap, it was a discussion with Alf Morris, who was expressing concern about the persistence of negative attitudes towards the disabled and wondering how these might be improved, that stimulated the small piece of research described in this book.

ATTITUDES, RELATIONSHIPS, AND SYSTEMS

Those of us who have some acquaintance with social psychology will know that attitudes – what they are, how they form, and how they change – have been a central and fertile topic for research, experimentation, theorizing, argument, and debate for half a century. Yet, despite all this effort, it can hardly be said that there is a coherent and consistent body of knowledge that could be applied to the kind of issue that Alf Morris was concerned with.

Textbooks on the subject – and there are scores of them – typically begin with a definition formulated by the American psychologist G. W. Allport in 1935. An attitude, he said, is:

'a mental and neural state of readiness, organized through experience, exerting a directive or dynamic influence upon the individual's response to all objects and situations with which it is related'.

(Allport 1935)

This definition and others of the same ilk are open to criticism for being too general and not discriminating sufficiently between 'attitudes', 'beliefs', 'feelings', 'values', 'habits', etc. The textbooks will then explore possible differences among these concepts and discuss the merits or otherwise of making fine distinctions. This becomes relevant when one turns to measurement. The construction and validation of tests and scales has been a thriving specialism, but we are ultimately left with the same unsatisfactory ambiguity as in attempts to measure intelligence; tests cannot measure intelligence; we can say only that an individual scores high or low on a particular test; and hence we have to resort to defining 'intelligence' (firmly in quotation marks) as whatever it is that the tests measure. In the case of attitudes, all that we can measure are a person's oral or written responses to a set of questions. Two difficulties stand out. First, the items that the investigator selects for his questionnaire and the way in which he formulates them will be an expression of his own attitudes, his own way of looking at the world, and this will not necessarily correspond to the picture that the subjects have in their heads. Second, the subject will inevitably be responding not only to the question but to the image he has of the investigator. Will I then be expressing my 'real' attitudes or what I want you to think I think – or maybe what I think you think I ought to think? Social psychologists have been trying to find ways round these difficulties. For example, repertory grid techniques allow the subject to develop his own 'personal construct' instead of having to respond to the construct of the investigator (cf. Kelly 1955, Bannister and Mair 1968, Bannister 1977, Fransella and Bannister 1977).

One other disappointing feature of research in this field is that measured attitudes are unreliable as a guide to predicting behaviour. By and large, psychologists concerned with attitude measurement have steered clear of behaviour:

'Direct observation of natural behaviour towards an attitude object is not only difficult and time consuming but only provides a measure which, because of the influence and constraints imposed by other factors, is likely to be difficult to interpret as well.'

(Stevens 1975: 18)

Sometimes the discrepancies are striking. In one study of nurses, an overwhelming majority in a control sample – 10 out of 12 – asserted that they would never accept a prescription from an unknown doctor and would always check the correct dosage before administering a medicine. In the experimental sample, each nurse received a telephone call from an unknown 'doctor' asking her to give a drug (in fact, a placebo, though its use was unauthorized) to a particular patient in a quantity exceeding the indicated dose. Ninety-five per cent of the nurses complied (Hofling *et al.* 1966). The ethics of this experiment were questionable; but even so the results were dramatic.

The relationship between attitudes and behaviour is also problematic in another respect. We tend to think of attitude change as preceding behavioural change; but while this may be the normal process, it has been suggested that the opposite may also occur: 'gradual shifts in perceptual structure, aided by repetition, activated by behavioural choice situations and *followed* at some time by attitude change' (Krugman 1965, quoted by Halloran 1967: 117–18). Halloran (himself a sociologist), after reviewing the writings of social psychologists bearing on attitude formation and change, concluded that what was needed was a broader perspective:

'It is . . . important to remember that there is more to behaviour than attitudes. We are faced with a problem area which involves inter-relationships between the various components in a social structure. The concern is with institutions, norms, attitudes, values and behaviour; in short with people and their social activities in society. Consequently, some thought must be given to the formulation of a sociological model which will facilitate the fitting together of the many discrete findings into an integrated social structure and process. In the long run, an attempt must be made to organize the relevant available pieces of

9

substantive knowledge in terms of the relevant theories of
social systems.' (Halloran 1967: 119)

We ourselves, not being social psychologists, pondered on
Alf Morris's concern on the basis of our own experience in the
field of disability. Between us, separately and jointly, we had
been involved in a series of action research projects conducted
at the Tavistock Institute from 1966 onwards. Themes we had
worked on included: residential care of the physically handicapped and chronic sick; geriatric hospital care; the
psychological needs of small children spending long periods in
an orthopaedic hospital; social rehabilitation of patients in a
hospital for the mentally handicapped; and the processes of
introducing innovations in patient care in a psychiatric
hospital.[2]

We and our colleagues had come from a variety of disciplines
– clinical psychology, psychoanalysis, social anthropology,
sociology, history, statistics – and this in itself prevented our
viewing phenomena through a single optic, such as attitudes.
Moreover, action research itself obliged us to try to enlarge the
understanding of the groups we were working with in these
various settings, so whatever hypotheses we produced had to
be cast in a form that might be useful to them. We were into an
'enlightenment' model of social research (cf. Janowitz 1966;
Miller and Gwynne 1972: 6.). Essentially this meant starting
from a study of behaviour – what people were actually doing
and their own descriptions of it. Human problems, as has been
pointed out often enough, do not fit neatly into the compart-
ments of scientific disciplines; so we had to find ways of

[2] Other Tavistock Institute staff involved in these projects were, principally,
Isabel Menzies, Penny Jones, David Towell, and Sheila Scott. We worked in
various configurations:
physical handicap: Gwynne and Miller;
geriatric hospitals: Dartington, Gwynne, Jones, Miller, and Scott;
orthopaedic hospital: Dartington and Menzies;
mental handicap: Dartington, Jones, and Miller;
psychiatric hospital: Miller and Towell.
Relevant publications include: Miller and Gwynne (1972), Miller and
Gwynne (1973), Miller (1975), Dartington and Miller (1977), Towell and
Harries (1979), Miller (1979), Dartington (1979), Dartington (1980),
Towell and Dartington (1976), Towell (1979). These projects, like the one
reported here, all received funding from the DHSS.

describing, understanding, and explaining behaviour that made sense both to ourselves and to the client groups, and, in addition, gave them some leverage for thinking about possible change.

This last point is perhaps worth emphasizing. The fact that we were analysing and interpreting behaviour in no way implied that we were taking up the 'behaviourist' position of trying to change other people. Our aim – not always achieved – was to illuminate what they were doing and why it seemed they were doing it, so that they themselves could make up their minds about whether and what to change. Nonetheless, we were undeniably interested in change, partly from the theoretical point of view – it nearly always helps to illuminate how systems actually work – and partly for the more humane reason that in the health and social services there is always scope for improving the lot of patients and clients.

The fact that we were focusing on actual behaviour and not starting from any specific discipline did not mean that we had embarked on these earlier studies with minds that were intellectually blank. One framework that we had found and continue to find useful in a comprehensive range of other institutional settings – not only in health and welfare but, for example, in education, religion, industry, commerce, agriculture, government, public administration, and voluntary service – was derived from the theory of open systems (cf. Miller and Rice 1967; Miller and Gwynne 1972; Miller 1977). Groups and institutions (and indeed individuals) can be conceptualized as social systems whose distinctive patterns of behaviour are a product of both internal and external forces. A second framework, drawn from psychoanalysis, enabled us to interpret the behaviour of individuals and larger systems as having both conscious and unconscious elements. In the realm of human action, of course, effects often diverge from intentions. We consider the discrepancies worth examination. Thus, if a set of people consistently profess that they are setting out to do one thing and equally consistently produce an outcome that bears little relation to what they say, then we can postulate that their behaviour is unconsciously motivated.

Going back to the earlier quotation from Stevens, therefore, we agree that 'direct observation of natural behaviour towards an attitude object' *is* difficult, and it certainly does not produce readily quantifiable results; but we nevertheless regard it as imperative. In particular, it introduces a concept that is not readily accommodated in attitude testing – the concept of ambivalence. Feelings aroused by an 'object' – a person, a group, an idea – are often contradictory. Sometimes we deal with this by the simple expedient of splitting the feelings and suppressing the one that we believe would be unacceptable in a given social situation. Among my liberal friends I argue for unrestricted immigration; among my neighbours I share the hope that no blacks will ever come to live in *our* street. But if the feelings evoked and the contradictions between them are too strong, then the individual may not be able to bear this ambivalence: the unacceptable feeling is split off and repressed. Such a disowned, unconscious feeling may then find expression in oblique ways – for example, by being projected into others. I idealize blacks and bitterly condemn my neighbours for their prejudice.

Our attention to actual behaviour and alertness to unconscious processes means that, in our usage, the term 'attitude' has certain overtones which are absent in the writings of many social psychologists. One part of the use is fairly straightforward and conventional: an attitude is the guiding definition of his relationship to the 'other' that the individual uses in order to reconcile the feelings that he has towards the other with the norms of the social system that prescribes what beliefs and behaviour are appropriate (Katz 1960). He will be able to state his definition more or less explicitly. The other part is the attitude inferred from his behaviour. It, too, is related to feelings, but the feelings may not be conscious and the definition so inferred may not be one that the individual is happy to own.

Put that way, our usage does indeed sound complex. Yet it is not very different from ordinary, everyday parlance. If I say, 'He has an odd attitude towards . . .', I may mean, 'What he *says* is odd' – i.e. his professed attitude is deviant from social norms – or alternatively I may mean, 'What he *does* is odd', in which case I am inferring his attitude, as we commonly do, from his behaviour.

Approaching the Study of Attitudes

This, in brief, was the background against which we began to tackle Alf Morris's question about attitudes: a set of action research projects and the use (though not exclusively) of a particular intellectual framework. In the next section we pick out the main themes from this earlier work that seemed to be relevant.

THEMES FROM EARLIER WORK

Mixed and conflicting feelings were a phenomenon that we were very much aware of in ourselves from the outset of the first of these studies, that of institutions for the physically handicapped:

> 'We found ourselves subjected to pronounced oscillations of feeling. One day we would be overwhelmed with sympathy and pity for the plight of the disabled, doubly persecuted by their physical handicaps and by the destructiveness of the environment in which they lived. Next day we would see the staff as victims of the insistent, selfish demands of cripples who ill-deserved the money and care that were being so generously lavished upon them. . . .'
>
> (Miller and Gwynne 1972: 7–8)

Our open confession of ambivalence got us into trouble in some quarters: if we held attitudes that were so plainly outdated and wrong, how could our analysis of residential care be taken seriously (cf. Hunt 1972)? We have nevertheless continued to believe that we are not unique in our ambivalence and that human societies have always had acute difficulty in coping with damaged members. 'Membership' and 'damage' are somehow irreconcilable. Anthropological evidence of the various social devices that are used would support the notion of a basic, primitive wish to extrude – even destroy – the damaged member; running against this wish, and perhaps arousing guilt about feeling it, are the obligations of family and fellowship; and a variety of mechanisms have been devised to defend societies and their members against the anxiety produced by this ambivalence. Through these mechanisms, reciprocal rights and obligations and proper patterns of behaviour are defined in a way that usually places the cripple at a greater

13

social distance. In most instances he is assigned a lower status; in a few societies he is treated with exceptional respect; but rarely – very rarely indeed – is he treated as ordinary.

In our own society, social distancing is often reinforced by physical distancing: handicapped people are 'put away' in special institutions; there are still instances of urban residents petitioning against proposed new local units – 'not in our street' – and in fact a lot of residential establishments are located a long way from civilization. In *A Life Apart* we suggested that this is because the inmates of these institutions are more than just crippled: effectively they have been written off by society, as if they no longer have membership in it. Hence the implicit task of the institution is to cater for the 'socially dead' in the interval in between social and physical death.

Segregation protects the general public from being confronted by the damage and the feelings it evokes; but it is only partly successful in protecting the inmates themselves from the negative attitudes towards them. These attitudes are imported into the institution, by managing bodies, by staff, and indeed by residents, as well as impinging on it from outside. Because the implicit task is too painful to confront directly, compensatory defensive task definitions and structures emerge which may partly mitigate the pain, but at some cost.

One such structure we identified as 'the humanitarian defence'. It is difficult to argue against the view that severely handicapped inmates need to be treated and cared for in ways that will preserve and prolong their lives – or, to put it in another way, postpone their physical death for as long as possible. This humanitarian value lies at the base of our medical and nursing professions, to whom we entrust the task of dealing with damaged members of society in general. It is associated, however, with the hope and expectation, within these professions and outside, that the damage can be repaired. That is their source of satisfaction and our criterion of their competence and success. Applied in these institutions, where the damage is not repairable, it leads to what we called the 'warehousing model' of residential care, which is a transfer into the residential setting of the values, structures, and defences of the hospital (cf. Menzies 1960). The patient or inmate is defined in terms of his or her physical malfunctioning; effective performance of the task requires the patient to be dependent and, often, depersonalized:

> 'any attempts by the inmate to assert himself, or to display individual needs other than those arising from his specific disability, are in the warehousing model constraints on task performance. They are therefore to be discouraged. The "good" inmate is one who accepts the staff's diagnosis of his needs and the treatment they prescribe and administer.'
>
> (Miller and Gwynne 1972: 86)

For those who have to staff these institutions, and still more for the rest of us who consign people to them, it is reassuring to feel that the inmates are getting the best of physical care and perhaps their lives are being prolonged. The assumption is that they will be grateful and contented. The possibility that their lives may be unfulfilled and unhappy is one that we prefer not to entertain.

The 'liberal defence' stands the humanitarian philosophy on its head. It is, if anything, anti-medical. The emphasis is not on the damage but on the person, the fellow-member of society. The inmate is 'really normal', with the same rights as everyone else for autonomy, self-development, and self-fulfilment. Flowing from this set of values is the 'horticultural model' of the residential institution, in which – if we conceptualize the institution as an open system – the intake into the system is defined as a deprived individual with unfulfilled capacities, and the primary task is to develop this potential. Hence the proper role of staff is not to treat the disability but to provide opportunities for the growth of ability. We were hesitant about labelling this as a defence and were lambasted for doing so (e.g. Hunt's review); but our reasons were twofold. First, emphasis on development seemed to be associated with denial of disability and thus with unrealistic fantasies of rehabilitation: if the handicapping effects could be overcome, the disability itself would somehow go away. Second, related to this, the ideology of independence called for an autonomy and a capacity for self-fulfilment greater than most 'really normal' people have, while the dependence on others, which all of us have and which those who are physically handicapped have

15

more than most, was defined as a weakness. Both models had to be classified as defences since they shied away from the societal definition of 'social death' and they related only to one aspect of the crippled inmates: either the damage or the (really normal) person. Hence the posture they valued was either dependence or independence. Residential institutions, as we perceived them, found it difficult to relate to their inmates *both* as damaged *and* as people, *both* as dependent *and* as independent. Out of this work we proposed a model of residential care within which the two aspects could be acknowledged and brought together and, in particular, inmates could acquire a bigger role in managing transactions across the boundary between the institution and its environment.

Some of the criticisms levelled against this piece of work were valid, some less so. The fact that we described what seemed to be happening did not mean that we approved of it; but the messenger always runs the risk of being shot. On the other hand, there were also favourable comments and the study has been described as an 'influential contribution to understanding what needed to be done, how and by whom in many residential situations' (Younghusband 1978, II: 177). The design of one new institution, described in Chapter 3, was explicitly based on the 'open system' model we had put forward, which showed the link between internal quality of life and external relations with the environment. Recent guidelines for caring for long-stay patients in hospital similarly use a norm of human interaction outside the hospital as the criterion for the quality of life to be attained within (Elliot 1975). In addition, the book helped to fuel a growing movement to find effective alternatives to institutional care.

The relationship of institutional to community care has its own problems. We had found in that first study that institutions used their admission criteria as a defence against having to face the human problems involved in selection and rejection, and we developed this hypothesis further in the subsequent study of hospital care of another disadvantaged category in society, the elderly. We again found ambivalent attitudes of maintaining independence and also responding to dependence in people who had already experienced a sort of 'social death'. The geriatric problem was apparently insoluble – old people would not get younger – and those involved in different caring systems would act out the unresolved conflicts between therapeutic and custodial objectives by taking sides, within and between hospital and community care systems. While each of these systems would seem to be carrying out its task in a reasonable way, it maintained the reasonableness at some cost through the process of referral to other systems. In the process, the referring system would try to present to the potential receiving system a picture of the patient or client that was calculated to make him or her acceptable to the recipient. Such a picture underlined some characteristics, and edited out others: it was partial in both senses of the word. Consequently, the overall provision of care to the elderly, as they were passed between these systems, was undermined.

From this and the further study that we made in a hospital for the mentally handicapped, we concluded that the more a social problem seems to be intractable, the more the specialized agencies mobilize to fragment it. Its intractabilities are then split off and projected from one agency to another. In this way, more widely held and diffused attitudes towards the handicapped are focused in the behaviour of the different interest groups, in both the formal and the informal networks of community care.

The trend away from custodial care has not done away with the need for formal institutions, but social isolation is no longer such an obvious requirement of formal care. Hostels and other units of care are located in the 'community' – i.e. where other people live. The group and intergroup dynamics of the total institution are diffused in the different environment of informal helping networks. We argued that institutions for the physically handicapped and chronic sick have as their primary task to cater for the socially dead between social death and physical death. Community care, on the other hand, implies non-acceptance of social death. Hence structural and cultural mechanisms for coping with feelings about damage and death, for these and other similarly disadvantaged sets of people, have to be worked out in extended networks of systems which include professional workers in health and social services.

In short, we concluded from these earlier studies that a significant dynamic, which interferes with an appropriate response to the handicapped, whether in residential or community care, is the splitting of ambivalent feelings among different individuals and groups in a support system or set of systems. These then act out the different feelings in conflictual or blocked relationships – usually at the expense of the very people, the handicapped themselves, whom the systems were created to support.

THE HYPOTHESIS AND THE RESEARCH

Our proposition, based on this experience, was that attitudes cannot be understood only at the level of the individual, or even of the particular role he may occupy in relation to disabled people: to some extent the attitudes he mobilizes are a function of the operation of other attitudes elsewhere in a given network or system of relationships around the disabled. To use a very simple example, idealization of the disabled in one part of a system and rejection in another may be seen as sustaining each other. Or – to go back to a point made earlier in this chapter – the greater the tolerance and understanding I display towards the other, the more he may need to resort to extreme behaviour in order to assert his difference and separateness from me.

It seems that often a double assumption is being made – that the problem lies in *negative* attitudes and that these are held by *other* people. We began to argue that it may be useful to turn this formulation upside down and to think about modifying *positive* – perhaps excessively positive – attitudes which might be reinforcing negative attitudes elsewhere (Dartington and Miller 1977). We were putting forward, in other words, the notion of a *distribution* of attitudes within these systems or networks. If that could be more fully demonstrated, then it seemed likely that attempts to change attitudes would not only be difficult but might even have negative consequences elsewhere. Could we more usefully think therefore about a creative *re*distribution of attitudes?

One obvious difficulty is that any given system of reciprocally reinforcing attitudes will be resistant to efforts at redistribution. However, certain roles may be identified as exercising a boundary function in the management of attitudes. For example, Goffman (1963) refers to 'the wise' –

non-stigmatized persons who are closely related to a stigmatized group and act as its representatives and advocates. Almost every account of the effects of handicap, in describing how those relating with the disabled interpret them to a wider society and interpret that society to the handicapped group, makes implicit or explicit reference to the role of the professional (e.g. Davis 1961; Scott 1974). Although the professional is of central importance here, the interpretative role may be taken in other ways: as Dartington (1971) has shown in his study of Task Force, for example, a voluntary organization may take on a similar role in relation to a handicapped group – in this case the elderly – and to a professional agency. One further proposition, therefore, is that in any given system or network of relationships, and thus of attitudes, around the disabled, there are certain roles that are either expressly or implicitly concerned with management of attitudes within that system, and that the occupants of these roles are potential 'action levers' in securing a redistribution of attitudes. We thought, too, that in these roles we were especially likely to locate some of the uncritically positive attitudes.

These then were the propositions we were trying to put to a preliminary test. As in previous studies, we decided to use the methods of action research, because the research worker's obligation to feed back his understandings to the client group as he goes along means that he has to formulate his working hypotheses in a way that bears directly on their experience in their roles. Also, we hoped that changes occurring in such a client system, as we worked with it, might give us further evidence about the processes of distribution and redistribution of attitudes.

We were fortunate in finding groups of people who were not only willing to work with us in this way but in two cases (where institutional identities would have been difficult to disguise) to expose themselves to a wider reading public. Such willingness reflects, we believe, quite a widespread concern among people in and around the world of the physically disabled to find appropriate attitudes and ways of behaving, so as to reconcile their own feelings and anxieties with social values that are ambiguous and shifting. Representatives of the main collaborating groups, some physically disabled themselves and

19

some not, also met in a one-day seminar (hosted by the King's Fund) towards the end of our project. That turned out to be an occasion not only for us to get some of our emerging ideas aired and examined but also to experience yet again, in a live setting, the processes of attitude distribution.

OUTCOMES

We think we enlarged the understanding of some of the people we worked with, though by no means all. We certainly enlarged our own. The concept of attitude distribution is now more sharply delineated. We have been able to identify what turns out to be a surprisingly small number of 'attitudinal sets' or 'constructs', which structure the vast majority of transactions with and around the physically disabled, and to show how they are related to each other. We have not been able to offer a clear-cut example of planned redistribution of attitudes: how far we have demonstrated its feasibility it must be left to the reader to judge.

Chapter 2, 'Reality and the Ideal', is an account of work with a committee charged with setting up a housing project for the disabled and with recruiting candidates for the new accommodation from existing residential institutions. Chapter 3 records something of the excitement and difficulties of starting up a new and innovative residential establishment in a London housing estate. (The chapter is called 'Authority and Power', but an alternative title might be 'Beyond the Horticultural Model'.) Chapter 4 focuses more directly on the handicapped in the community. It draws on several other settings in which we worked during the research and takes us into the fields of employment (with particular emphasis on the role of disabled resettlement officers); other kinds of work and occupation (e.g. day centres); housing; and leisure (including clubs and a holiday for the handicapped at which one of us took the role of attendant for a week). In the last chapter we attempt a somewhat more theoretical formulation. Social psychologists will probably find it unsatisfactory and it does not really succeed in answering Alf Morris's question; but if it provides a little more illumination for those who have to move in this complex area we shall be content.

2
Reality and the ideal

THE ORIGINS OF A COMMUNITY CARE SCHEME FOR SEVERELY
DISABLED CEREBRAL PALSIED, DEVELOPED BY THE SPASTICS
SOCIETY

BACKGROUND

In thinking about possible sites for our study, we were aware
that the new town of Milton Keynes was perhaps offering an
environment that would have advantages for disabled
living: new housing stock, a comprehensive system of path-
ways separate from motor traffic, encouragement to
community initiatives, and, symbolically, a city centre on one
level, with wheelchairs available to shoppers on demand.

In discussions with the Development Corporation, we heard
of one scheme in particular; a housing estate, Neath Hill, was
under construction, with twenty-four flats specially adapted to
the needs of disabled people. These flats were to be scattered
throughout the estate, and the Spastics Society was proposing
to use them to house cerebral palsied adults, who otherwise
would have to remain in the Society's residential centres or
other institutional care. Also there was to be a 'professional
workshop' for twelve highly qualified disabled people, of
whom at least six would be cerebral palsied.

The Spastics Society agreed to our attending the meetings of
their co-ordinating committee for the new project, and the
applications group reviewing potential residents; it was also
possible to interview the residents when they were accepted. In
this way, we were able to observe the development of the
project: it was hoped that residents would be living in the new
housing during the time of our study, but delays meant that we
were to concentrate on the work towards realizing the
community care scheme but not to see it in action.

The project was an amalgamation of two ideas: for 'Fokus'

21

housing on the Swedish model,[1] and for the 'professional workshop', where the participants could create their own business and commercial opportunities for work. Eighteen of the twenty-four flats would be for one or two people, and were interspersed among standard tenant-occupied premises. Six would be for single persons and these would be grouped near the professional workshop and reserved for its workers. Each flat would have a bedroom, sitting/dining room, kitchen, and bathroom. They were to be centrally heated and have their own double carport leading to a small garden. The whole of Neath Hill was planned to be accessible to those in wheelchairs. The pavements would be ramped and the shops designed so that disabled tenants had access. The Spastics Society intended to provide a transport service for tenants so that they could make use of the facilities of the new city.

In order that tenants might lead independent integrated lives within the community, it would be necessary to ensure that suitable assistance was available as and when required. Under the guidance of an organizer, and a small number of full-time staff, part-time general assistants would be employed from the local community and given basic training in the handling of the disabled. The flats would be linked by an extensive communications system, including a two-way intercom, with two staff houses in the area. This would ensure that sufficient assistance was available for tenants during peak demand periods. There would also be a permanently manned control panel to answer calls throughout the whole twenty-four-hour period.

All potential residents for the special housing scheme were to undergo a period of training and assessment in special flats at a Spastics Society hostel. This would help all concerned to understand and overcome some of the problems of living on their own. The whole scheme was to be Part 3 accommodation, that is to say tenants would still be classified as technically in residential care and sponsored by their local authorities. The

---

[1] We were often asked during our research what we thought of 'Sweden', as if this were a litmus paper of attitudes. Significantly, this was also the starting-point of the first set book for the Open University course (Brattgard, in Boswell and Wingrove 1974).

fees charged to the authorities would be no higher than those at the ordinary residential centres of the Spastics Society.

The professional workshop would provide office accommodation for up to twelve participants, with secretarial and administrative facilities available to each participant as required. Each would be encouraged to develop his own business or clientele dependent upon his individual skills, and specialized equipment would be made available. Participants in the workshop had to be either graduates or people with equivalent ability. This included people with appropriate professional qualifications, and those whose IQ was above 120. The balance within the group of interests and abilities would be very important and this aspect would be considered very carefully when choosing the initial participants. All members of the workshop had to be prepared to work a thirty-hour week on projects which would earn money. When necessary participants had to be prepared to work in groups with other members of the professional workshop. This would particularly apply where expensive specialist installations were involved in order to obtain a reasonable amount of use from the equipment. It was anticipated that half of the members of the workshop would be cerebral palsied and the remainder would have a range of different non-progressive conditions. All the tenants in the housing scheme were to be cerebral palsied. At the time of our study, the task for the co-ordinating committee was to work out the practical details of the project.

FROM 'RESIDENTIAL' CARE TO 'COMMUNITY' CARE

The idea of what was to become the Milton Keynes Community Care Service appealed strongly to senior administrators of the Spastics Society. When the time came to publicize the scheme to residents of the existing residential centres, they were personally involved in encouraging residents to think of applying. They emphasized the opportunities opened up by 'living in the community'. Their visits to the residential units are remembered by staff there for the almost evangelical quality of their 'campaign'. In contrast, those working in the centres naturally had their doubts about the viability of the idea. After all, they felt that they knew their residents and understood the limits of their potential for independent living. It was the dependence of their residents, physical and psychological, that was central to their experience.

Here was a situation of potential conflict. A, in his role, is looking for ways of extending and developing the overall possibilities of care provision for the cerebral palsied. B, in his role, is doing his best to provide care according to an existing model of residential care for which he is held responsible. Because of these differences of perspective, we can see how A and B may draw on different sets of attitudes and values influencing their actions and reactions in circumstances new to both of them. We see the function of roles in the distribution of attitudes.

A is interested in an exciting new idea which links with a view of the severely disabled as really normal, able to live in their own homes, to be responsible for their own lives, to have privacy and personal autonomy as well as the necessary care. These are ideals which, if realized, help to confirm us in our view that the disabled, despite limitations of physical functions, can take on an active social role. So A is working to an attitudinal set that emphasizes the idea of the disabled as really normal. But is he doing more than accepting the disabled as normal? He has invested effort in working towards the circumstances that the disabled, at present socially disenfranchized, might better meet his idea of them as socially normal. He is representing an idea of what might be realistic as a different position from what is presently realistic. At the moment, he cannot see the disabled simply as normal, for he is also still responsible for a system of care that is segregated and containing and based to some extent on a warehousing model. His enthusiasm overrides that present reality. He becomes more of a patron of the disabled, in the old-fashioned sense of the word. He takes up the position that we may think of as enlightened guardianship.

This leaves B with an ill-defined sense of unease. His responsibilities to the immediate management for the care of residents puts him in the position of defining reality – what is possible and what is not – according to his own experience within the constraints of existing resources. But in that system, he may be attempting to find an appropriate balance between the warehousing and horticultural models of institutional care. If questioned about current practice in the care that he manages, he is likely to argue that it meets the needs of the residents. His position is of somebody fixed in the present reality, as he defines that reality.

His attitudinal set therefore is in his own terms positive and constructive. Faced with the challenge posed by the idealism of the new scheme, unrealistic in his own eyes, he seems to be drawing on an attitude that says that disabled people are not quite whole, and the more he feels the pressure to lay down realistic limits, the more he appears to be emphasizing the disabilities rather than the abilities of those for whom he is taking up a representative role. In his own eyes, he feels unfairly under attack. To others, he may now seem to be conservative and unimaginitive. He justifies his position by looking at the aspirations of the residents in his care. From his perspective, any resident who wants to leave residential care and go to the new scheme is potentially deviant. By definition, such a resident is unrealistic, because he is applying to live in an unrealistic scheme.

In this analysis, we are not saying that A is right or more right than B, or that B is right or more right than A. If it is possible to suspend judgement for a time, we can see the extent to which judgements are based on attitudes associated with our own roles in relation to the disabled.

Developing an alternative scheme of care may be seen as a transition from the idea to the new reality. It is not only the road to hell that is paved with good intentions. In fact one of the factors inhibiting growth may be that allowance has to be made for the giving up of aspects of what was ideal in order to make do with what has actually been achieved. In such a process, characterized by shifts in perceptions of reality, those in different roles have to shuffle and reshuffle the attitudinal sets by which they work.

For example, in articulating ideas, we immediately come up against problems of definition. What do we actually mean by 'living in the community'? As our definitions of community are likely to be vague, so we may not know what we mean by living in it, whatever it is, but we do know that it is different from living in an institution! Talking of living in the community is 'a good thing'; it is a way of laying claim to certain attitudes which are thought to be positive. So faced with attacks on their isolationism, those responsible for institutional care have come to emphasize the open boundaries of what they are doing. It may be an institution but it is part of the community. Moreover, there is more real community in this way, it can be argued, than is achieved by putting people out in the community as isolated individuals. Forced into a position of justifying institutional care, with its implications that people are socially stunted, the managers of residential care change the argument. Those living in the community are then the deprived, for that community is then seen as an isolating, impoverished environment, to be compared negatively with the caring society of the institution. These arguments are maddening and inconclusive. They are evidence though of a search for a position that is internally consistent.

'Living in the community' with reference to the Milton Keynes project was intended to mean that people could live in their own homes and yet receive the care that they needed and had got in institutional life. This idea, appealing to A in the role of innovatory management, leant heavily on the attitudinal standpoint that the disabled are really normal. As an idea it suffered at an operational level. Those implementing the scheme were working within the constraints of their existing definitions of realistic provision for the disabled. But they tried to come to terms with a new 'reality'. This was in conflict with that part of their attitudinal set which saw the disabled as not whole.

The co-ordinating group was set up to manage this overall process, with an applications group, in effect a sub-committee of the main group, to look at potential residents. As the group as a whole had to hold on to the idea consistent with innovatory management (role A) and also to implement this policy and to be directly responsible then for the practical management of the project (role B), it had to find a way of maintaining at the same time two conflicting positions or achieving some integration of opposites. In their debating of issues, individuals took on different roles at different times. But the roles reflected the distribution of attitudes: debates in the group were at one level an exploration of these attitudes and a search for an effective relationship between the various polarized positions.

It can be seen that the task undertaken by the group required it to take on itself an active role of what has been called enlightened guardianship. Within that role there is no stable, straightforward, unambiguous attitudinal position to take. It can only be teased out and negotiated in relation to other positions by associating with some of them and opposing others. And perhaps it can never find more than a temporarily viable form.

Furthermore, the group representing an enlightened guardianship model on behalf of the Society was made up of individuals with other pre-existing roles within the Society. The chairman of the group was responsible for the residential centres from which the applicants were hoping to move. The group did not have a project manager whose task was to implement a new scheme. As it was, those involved were having to manage for themselves the boundary around this new project insofar as it differed from the rest of their work. However, two members of the group were appointed directly to work on the new scheme: one to manage the care and the other to set up the workshop for disabled who were professionally able to work. They did not have a divided allegiance and at times their frustration with the delays caused by constraints in implementing the scheme was more evident than that of other members of the group. The others were still responsible for the management of different aspects of the existing services of the Society.

In working as it did, the group had to keep on examining individually and collectively the nature of the boundary around the project in its relationship to the wider activities of the Society. What were they trying to do that was different from what they had been doing? Defining the task was done by taking up one position in distinction to another. Role A attitudes made people feel uncomfortable about what they were already doing but were legitimized by the attempt to do something different. Other, Role B, attitudes still had their expression in the maintenance of existing services.

The group was thus subject to outside pressures. Apart from

the relationship to the existing system of care, there was also the Development Corporation making available the new housing and the local authorities who were already providing the fees for residents in existing centres and would have to provide the fees for the new scheme. What happened then was that the authorities who potentially represented constraints on the realizing of the ideal became in psychological terms 'bad objects'. Those individuals who were working to realize the ideal were able to project on to others any difficulties to do with their own adjustment to a different way of working. In this way they could dispose of some of their own doubts and uncertainties and justify their own feelings of frustration. Outsiders had to be convinced of the viability of the new idea, and did not already have an investment in making the new idea work.

Local authorities – specifically their social services departments – are responsible for the provision of care for disabled people from their areas. Often they place people in residential care outside their territory, but they retain statutory responsibility to assess and monitor any care being given. From the perspective of the group, the authorities were, potentially at least, a constraining influence on an exercise that would do well by the disabled people, that would improve their quality of life. The local authorities had to be satisfied that their disabled people would get appropriate care in the new housing, compared to residential establishments. Yet in all discussions about negotiations with the local authorities, no time was taken with the need to demonstrate that there would be a better quality of life for the residents. The emphasis was entirely on being able to explain economic factors. The trump card seemed to be that the new scheme would not actually cost more. In fact, this was a guarantee that the Society was prepared to make: fees would not be greater than those currently being negotiated for existing residential care.

That the pressures were experienced as being about cost limits rather than quality control concerned this group in its enlightened guardianship role. Doubts that members of the group had about its attempts to push back the frontier of what was realistic for severely disabled, cerebrally palsied individuals, could to an extent be discounted; there were plenty of others who would carry such negative feelings. Often these others would be involved with issues which had nothing to do with disability and modes of care. For example, the authority that was releasing the housing – the MKDC – was inevitably caught up in the overall housing policy that it was responsible for, its contracts with builders, funding from the Department of the Environment, and so on. So uncertainties within the group about the feasibility of disabled residents becoming ordinary tenants did not need to be tested, so long as others could be construed as making it difficult for them to try out the positive ideal and to make it practicable.

These doubts about the disabled were more easily explored in the subgroup to do with the applications from potential residents. While the main committee were worried whether the scheme would be allowed to happen, the sub-group faced the other issue: assuming these constraints could be overcome, the residents would have to be able to take advantage of the opportunity that was being created for them for 'living in the community'.

The prospective residents were themselves having to rearrange their internal attitudinal sets as they adapted to the changed relationship of themselves to the care system of which they were also an integral part. Those who first applied for consideration to the housing scheme showed evidence both of independence of mind and dissatisfaction with their present circumstances. Several saw themselves implicitly as pioneers. Others were identified as 'restless'.

The applicants themselves were therefore likely to be in an ambivalent position. At one level they might be thought difficult (even deviant, according to the perspective of the immediate management in their care role B), and at another they might be perceived as élite in relation to the new project, to which there was a lot of prestige attached (this having to do with the management of innovation, Role A). The ambivalence of their position arose from the distribution of attitudes around them. In their existing homes they were exposed to an attitudinal set consistent with the management of their care. Thus the limitations of that care were seen in that context to be realistic and inevitable and not all that bad really. If the limitations of that care were to be taken as constant, then it was

29

a natural conclusion to see those limitations belonging inevitably to the disability of the individual. This attitude put a fixed boundary around the disabled individual. It said in effect, this is what you can do and no more.

Physical disability may be distinguished from a handi-capping environment (Wright 1960). But what was happening was arguably a confusion of the limitations of the environment with the disabilities of the individual. This confusion was perhaps unconscious but it had an important influence. It ensured that there was a reduction of any discordance between the individual and the environment: each was thought to be suited to the other.

THE ECONOMICS OF RESPONSIBILITY

The idea that disabled people might live independently in the community was subject to the most severe constraint of all, in that the residents moving into the housing in Milton Keynes were not responsible for their own financial survival. They were not to be responsible for their own rent, were not even to manage money provided through the social security system except for a small amount called 'pocket money' by the DHSS themselves and by the residents. Were the residents to remain financially impotent as well as dependent? It is true that in this case, the residents were to be responsible for their own domestic budgeting, including buying their own food. This in itself was a fundamental change and the three-month 'acclimatization' in self-contained flats in a hostel was largely taken up with adaptation to such changes. However, the residents were not paying rent. Social Services Departments, with which they had no contact, were paying fees to the Spastics Society, which was paying rent. Likewise, bills that were addressed to individual residents were not to be paid by the resident. While they might become aware of costs of heating, a part of life from which they had previously been protected, they were still not responsible for their payment of these bills. Much of the discussion in the co-ordinating group trying to determine its enlightened guardianship role had to be with defining where the responsibility of the quasi-tenant resident lay and where they, representing the Spastics Society, would remain ultimately responsible.

The fitting out of the flats, it was never questioned, was to be the responsibility of the Society. In fact they had little option on this. The residents could not have the financial independence to take on that responsibility themselves. Their 'income' came from fees payable by the local authorities. Unless they had private capital, they did not have anything beyond their 'pocket money'. The alternatives – residential care or 'living in the community' – of the new housing in Milton Keynes exposed the 'immaturity', the essential infantilization that goes almost without remark in the provision of care for severely disabled people, where they do not have control over their own financial affairs. Thus the attempt being made to offer independent living was inevitably frustrated by the statutory mechanisms through which residential care is financed.

For the members of the co-ordinating group, the implicit contradictions of their position in holding on to their enlightened guardianship meant that they were unable to feel happy with any financial forecasting about the costs of the scheme, so long as they were uncertain of the limits of individual responsibility of residents for their own living expenses. Time and again, they were faced with their own anxieties about budgetary control. It was perhaps inevitable that in the absence of independent project management these concerns became diffused in the wider issues of the financial costs of the whole operation of the Spastics Society and its residential care. This group would claim with some certainty that the fees of the new scheme would not be in excess of the fees of existing provision. But this was saying only that the Spastics Society's responsibility for the care of its residents in the new scheme would not be in excess of its responsibility in the settings from which these residents come. At this stage it was inevitable that the details of the costing were more a matter of faith than accountancy.

The group worked out a number of guidelines for a sharing of responsibility between the residents and the Society. For example, the Society would pay telephone rentals but residents would pay for call charges. Residents would buy their own clothing but there might be a call on a special fund where, for example, because of his disability, a resident had excessive shoe repairs. Residents would be able to bring in to their flats their own possessions. At the same time, the Society was concerned to get discounts on bulk purchases of furnishings appropriate to the need – carpets that could easily be cleaned, cupboards of a convenient size and so on. The residents would, of course, be able to quit – but they would have to wait for the Society to find them somewhere to go. It was less a matter of giving notice as applying for a transfer. All of this meant that the sharing of responsibility still left the Society ultimately responsible if things went wrong. The residents would be to a great extent protected from the consequences of their actions.

The question of ultimate responsibility was further explored with reference to the professional workshop. One of the rules of the workshop was to be that participants would be expected to work thirty hours a week. Were these thirty hours inclusive or exclusive of any physical care that they might require during that time? The participants were in a sense in tied housing. If they ceased to work at the workshop, would they then be required to leave the housing? How far were they subject to the ordinary insecurities of open employment or self-employment?

On this last point, there was a difficult issue to do with the financial viability of the workshop. The idea was that the workshop would become self-sufficient, that it would develop a commercial practice of some diversity and would compete commercially in the outside world. However, the setting-up costs would be met by the Society. Also the salary of the manager already appointed, and the capital cost of specialized equipment, including adaptation to meet the needs of the disabled participants would have to be met by the Society. At what point were the participants expected to take over? What about the depreciation? Was the manager to do himself out of a job after the initial setting-up period? What though if the workshop did not become commercially viable within the set period? In such ways, the group was having to find ways to meet the dependency needs of those who were disabled and, at the same time, demand that they stand on their own feet in their work expectations.

THE DISABLED IN TRANSITION

Disabled people accept limitations deriving from a diminished status and constraints on social as much as economic equality. This happens, for example, if they accept that they have to be in residential care. In accepting any kind of care, they make an implicit contract that the care is in their best interests. (Of course they may wish to question or change that contract but they must usually expect a hostile reaction if they do, with accusations that they are unrealistic/immature/not adjusted to their disability etc.) So residents may accept that they have very little private space, may be sharing a room, may prefer that because they are used to it and feel safe. According to a consensus model of disability, the disabled adapt to suit the resources available to them. It is therefore a matter of emotional and psychological significance that there be alternative resources available to those who have many years' experience of residential care. It is not simply that there might be some other place where they could live. There might be the opportunity to lead very different lives, to be in effect different people.

Procedures adopted by the Spastics Society made some allowance for this transition towards what one might call an open model of residential care, where people would be occupying their own living units in the community but receiving the same standards of physical care always previously required of an institution. Those who were thought likely to go to the new housing were able first to go to the hostel with its specially designed flats where they could experiment in independent living. This was also an opportunity for the Society to assess their needs in the changed circumstances that were envisaged for them. Generally speaking, applicants would spend three months at the hostel. The assessment of need for physical care was clearly important. There were, however, indications that this should not be seen as the primary task. Three months is perhaps generous for this task and certainly, at first, this formal assessment was not so thorough that in itself it explained the full significance of the event. The stay at the hostel seemed rather to be a kind of 'treat', an opportunity for people to review their own perceptions of their disability and so to work out a different frame of reference, by which they might make sense of living in the new housing scheme.

At this time, the applicants of the scheme were able to get away from the restrictions of residential care, as they understood it, but were not yet exposed to the 'freedom' of individual living as envisaged. So they were still subject to pressures in their past but also to the pressures of expectations about their future. In this context, the experience of the participants was by their own account a very good one. It may also have been disruptive in that it overturned some of their taken-for-granted assumptions, both about their limitations and about their potential. In fact part of what was 'good' may have been that it was disruptive.

To analyse the meaning of the experience – as a space where people could redefine themselves as disabled – we may outline some of the factors contributing to the making of that space.

1 References were taken up. Typically the referees were managers of the residential care from which applicants came, or social workers relating to them in that environment.

2 It was usually necessary, or at least politically sensible, to inform and get agreement from the local authority which was already paying fees for the residential care of the applicants. If accepted, these applicants would still be dependent on the authorities to pay their fees in the different setting. (They would not envisage that the fees would be increased but sponsoring authorities would retain the right to determine whether or not to approve the care received by the disabled for whom they retained responsibility.)

3 The applications group of the Society, itself holding a middle position between the old and the new, the past and the future, came to a decision on whether the applicants were potentially acceptable in the new housing.

Their criteria for making this judgement were not clear cut and they were aware that their role was in fact to be uncertain. They adopted a procedure, but knew that the taking up of references had to be understood in the context of the existing situation, while the assessment of potential was projected on to an uncertain future. They discussed in detail the issues around the individual, but in general their decisions were made more according to practical questions, and if the application was seriously made, they took the first step of approving the experiment of going to the hostel.

They then had a second task, to determine whether the hostel experiment was a success and to approve the application to go to the new housing. But this raised further issues about the viability of the scheme. At this stage too, decisions still had to be based on assumptions about the idea rather than on the reality. The reality was not yet there, no housing was yet available and those who completed their stay at the hostel returned meanwhile to the residential care from which they had come.

So, there was a first stage of transition that left those involved uncertain about what had actually changed. In this sense, the roles of both managers of care and residents were not neatly rounded off. Moreover, as we will see, the kind of psychological defences people used to explain themselves were also in a state of flux. In such a situation those managing the transition may hold simultaneously different attitudes in conflict: on the one hand, that disabled people are dependent and their needs have to be interpreted for them by their able-bodied protectors, and on the other, that they are able to function as social beings, including the making of the same mistakes as anyone else. The applicants were still clients, in a social sense, while they were learning to live more like tenants, ordinary citizens. Much of the debate about applicants had to do with seeing if it were possible to let go of them as clients and to allow them their rights as tenants.

We have seen that outside pressures, in fact, ensured that they were always in some sense clients and weakened their fragile potential status as tenants. But these pressures also served to highlight the ambivalences and contradictory elements in the attitudinal sets that people have to draw on in thinking about their appropriate relationship to disabled residents. In the applications group, different individuals might be worried that applicants would not be able to cope or should be referred for psychiatric assessment or had unreal expectations of how they were going to be able to live independently, but at the same time they questioned in what way these worries were relevant to the task in hand. They were responsible for the applicants but it was not appropriate to see the applicants simply as dependent on them. They had also to be aware that their own uncertainties about the success of the scheme might affect how they saw the applicants, so that they might project on to the applicants their own doubts about independent living by the disabled.

This is a dramatic example of the impossibility of finding a consistent position. The temporary standpoint is defined only by the drawing of coefficients from polarized and conflicting landmarks, that the disabled are not whole beings and yet they are really normal. The disabled applicants were also exploring what meaning they were putting on their new status as 'tenant' while they were continuing to relate as clients. Their behaviour reflected this dilemma. In general, when they returned to the places they had come from they showed a patient acceptance of their dependence there, but at the same time demonstrated increasing irritation at their lack of fit with those environments.

What then were the expectations that people had of the disabled going to the new housing? (1) They were pioneers prepared to have a go at the challenge of independent living. (2) They were self-sufficient and not dependent on institutional life for social meaning. (3) They were ambassadors, able to represent the Spastics Society and themselves to show the community that they were good neighbours.

These are all aspects of the disabled as good citizens offering a model of how it is possible to overcome handicap. And the careful screening by the Spastics Society indicated how much was invested in their success in this representational role. (4) They had to have the sponsorship of local authorities prepared to pay the necessary fees for their housing and physical care. (5) They were prepared to go through the long-drawn-out application phase and accept the authority of the Society in administering the scheme. To this extent they would be expected to accept the dependency of their disabled status (in contrast, say, with whose who have on their own initiative been able to live in the community). Achieving the balance of being able to take up the role of a good citizen without giving up the status of being a dependant on the voluntary society and the local authority was the subject of much debate within the co-ordinating committee during the preparatory months.

THE TENANTS' AGREEMENT

The issues and dilemmas were encapsulated well in the co-ordinating group's attempts at a written agreement for these 'tenants'. It culminated in the formal recognition that those going into the new scheme were not tenants at all. This was to be an alternative kind of residential care. The first draft explained that the residents would have their mobility allowance where applicable of £10 and social security money of £19.50. That was their income and their outgoings would be rent of £4.60. But these figures were dependent on circumstances. The rent was not to do with what was being provided, it was very much to do with what people were able to contribute. In that this whole notion of 'rent' was immediately undermined. A more accurate description that was adopted was 'contribution towards fees'. It seemed a detail, but as soon as there was this shift from tenants paying rent, it was difficult even to think of the people as tenants at all.

Each resident would be responsible for food, cleaning utensils, shoe-mending, dry cleaning, laundry bills, telephone calls, general household replacements for small items and those not included in the provisional inventory, maintenance and replacement of wheelchairs, electric or manual (that is, those not supplied by the Ministry), and so on. Such a list might well seem to be extending the responsibility of the individual, but it was difficult to do it. Some disabled people have special problems with cleaning, for example. Shoe-mending is a very heavy item for those who drag their feet. Laundry bills might be excessive. The group were aware that residents would, in some cases, need financial or practical help with those items.

In thinking about residents' responsibilities towards the paying of bills, the telephone bill was a separate issue, as they would be responsible for their own calls, but not for the rental. They would consult with the care organizer about payment; here was an attempt to balance the new responsibilities of residents with the continuing responsibility of the Spastics Society. In the draft, there was a reference to the care staff; that they would not use tenants' phones to make personal calls, and if asked tenants could refuse. This was amended: 'Staff may not use tenants' phones to make personal calls'. There seemed

37

to be underlying worry about how far the tenants would have full rights in their own homes and how far they would be subject to the needs of care staff.

Under 'complaints procedure', it was thought best to delete reference to complaints about any member of staff, as if this was assuming that this was where the complaints would be directed, and leave it simply as any complaints. A lot of these amendments raised the question of relationship of care staff to residents. For example, a sentence was to be inserted to the effect that tenants were asked to exercise normal economy, particularly in the case of heating, which could be very expensive. This caused quite a debate as to whether it would be possible for care staff to intervene or even insist on tenants making such economies, when they were not in the end going to be responsible for the bills.

The draft agreement went on to discuss services provided by staff: that they would visit tenants in their flats by prior arrangement; that they would carry out normal domestic tasks which tenants could not do for themselves, such as cleaning and cooking. Likewise, they would carry out personal care which can be done routinely: bathing, hairwashing, feeding. They would attend in an emergency when they were summoned by the intercom system, for toileting, falls, and other emergencies. They would come as soon as possible, but it was pointed out that this might take five or ten minutes, longer than people might be expected to wait in institutional care. Staff would be on duty for twenty-four hours a day, but at night there would only be two staff awake.

There was a section on visitors: tenants could accommodate them in their own flats. But then tenants would have to look after them. But they were not able in all ways to look after themselves, so how would they look after their visitors? This was a problem to be negotiated with the care organizer.

'All laundry which is done by staff must be marked clearly with the tenant's name to avoid loss.' It was obviously reasonable for staff to help people out, but this was beginning to look like a normal procedure for providing for individual clothing in institutions.

Televisions were not provided by the Spastics Society. One piece of 'freedom' was that residents would be responsible for rental charges and also for their own television licence.

The amendments to the first draft of this tenancy agreement were themselves indicative of the ambivalent nature of the scheme. For example, outgoings. We have seen that references to 'rent' would be taken out, as this did not fit with the reality. What the people paid would vary according to the local authority assessment and their outlay would therefore represent only a contribution towards rent, the bulk being paid by the Society and being recovered by fees from the local authority. Holiday and clothing allowances likewise would be variable for each tenant. These would be to do with the financial assessment of the residents and would be nothing specifically to do with their status in the scheme.

In the second draft, the financial matters were put as an appendix. The difference in social security received and contributions to fees was composed of pocket money, £3.90, housekeeping, £11. The concept of pocket money might seem inappropriate for adults living independent lives – but residents would expect it, and, as we have noted, this payment is so called by the DHSS. The financial provision had remained consistent with their being in residential care.

In the end the problems of terminology were symbolic of other fundamental difficulties in achieving a new relationship of disabled people to their environment, in accord with other models of care. The attempt to draft a tenancy agreement was frustrated by the fact that they were not tenants. Furthermore, they did not like the word 'residents', with its associations to residential care.

Even more complex were issues to do with 'termination of agreement'. As this would be not simply an individual responsibility but would affect the Society, it was necessary to inform the Head of Centres in writing of any intention to terminate the agreement. This would not affect the Society's responsibilities for continuing care; an alternative would have to be found. It was as if increased individual responsibility for residents also meant increased responsibility (and worry) for those administering their care.

A Life Together

The translation of an ideal towards its realization involves a continuous testing of the concepts by which we try to understand what we think is right in a given situation. 'Disabled people should be able to live in their own homes, the same as everyone else.' This is a 'really normal' statement. For those who are responsible for the provision of housing for the disabled, the statement has a particular importance. It challenges the basis on which they have been providing residential care. It has an appeal for them to the extent that they are themselves dissatisfied with the present position. In making this statement, they are temporarily distancing themselves from another kind of statement: 'Disabled people do best in a protective environment where their needs can be met most easily'.

Because they are aware of the difficulties of managing such a protective environment and have experienced how it can be controlling, emotionally impoverishing, and so on, they are attracted to the first idea, as a means of getting relief from the ambivalent feelings that threaten to eclipse the good value in the other. It is suggested that the attitudinal set here would include both kinds of statements, and for the moment those managing the transition were attracted to both in their roles of managers of care with a responsibility not only for maintaining the existing system but promoting innovation and change.

The co-ordinating group were having to speculate about ways in which the project was likely to develop. Sometimes they seemed to be concerned that they would be overrun by the demand; at other times they worried that they would be unable to find enough suitable people. These extremes, at first sight puzzling, may reflect an underlying duality in the representative role. It involves interpreting the outside world to the disabled, and also the disabled to the outside world. The residents had to be special, if they were to be offered an opportunity to show that they were like everyone else and could live ordinary lives. The potential applicants were both ordinary – therefore many? – and 'special' – perhaps difficult to find?

Assessment of potential residents had to balance these

40

'special' and 'ordinary' factors. Mr and Mrs Bridges went to the hostel to experiment with individual living in a flat. But they had marital problems and were thinking of separating. Their stay at the hostel gave them an opportunity to work out these problems but they caused some concern for the co-ordinating group. What could they do about contingency plans? They were accepting married couples, but could they give them the opportunity to split up? As the accommodation was allocated to the residents, it was difficult then to revert to single accommodation.

Another couple were hoping to get married. Miss Harkness was living at home with her parents. She was engaged to be married to Mr Lord who was already accepted to go to Milton Keynes. He did not know whether to accept as there were difficulties in getting local authority sponsorship for his fiancée. Miss Harkness was once engaged before, and there was an attempt then to get the local authority to sponsor her. At first she was turned down but the authority was re-considering the decision when the engagement was broken off. The family were reluctant to get sponsorship until they were sure that she would be accepted for Milton Keynes. But the Spastics Society were unwilling to consider her without informing the local authority; after all, they would then be expecting the authority to contribute fees. Even going to the hostel for assessment was problematic: usually a local authority was expected to contribute fees for that, to under-stand what it was intended to achieve, and understand what was going to be asked of it in the long term. The family offered to pay her fees to go to the hostel but that did not overcome the difficulty. In contrast, when Mr Lord had gone there: he had simply taken his social security money – about £11 a week; but that was because he came from residential care already. Miss Harkness had in fact stayed a week at Birmingham – as his guest.

The traditional focus of care was thus the disabled individual: as individuals achieved normal relationships, they were subject to new constraints on their freedom of action. Did Miss Harkness want to have a baby? Even the new project did not have accommodation for a *growing* family. Local authority sponsorship also focused on the individual. A married couple living in the same flat were to be sponsored separately, and their individual fees were each the same as for a single person occupying a similar space. The suggestion to charge a reduced fee in such circumstances was rejected on the grounds that local authorities might object to an 'increased' fee for single people.

It is a matter of opinion – highly relevant in the discussion of difficulties – whether the constraints on normal living – getting married, having babies and, it seems, getting divorced – are part of the reality of being disabled, or whether these constraints amount to discrimination, as defined by the Committee on Restrictions against Disabled People: 'the unjustified withholding, whether intentional or not, of some service, facility or opportunity from a disabled person because of that person's disability' (CORAD 1979).

It was evident that the new project was opening up such questions. In pushing back the boundaries of what was thought possible in provision for the severely disabled, it exposed more areas of concern in thinking about the ways that disabled are subject to the will of able-bodied representatives of their interest. For members of the applications sub-group, this was unsettling: starting from a benevolent position, they found that they were again having to apply restrictive 'reality' standards, often of the greatest importance to the lives of others.

But the basic idea of disabled people 'living in the community' is that the disabled people are just like the rest of us. We should not have to be frightened of them, guilty about them, or protective of them against ourselves. The care we provide is done with the best of intentions but all 'care' has side effects. It is worth looking at these effects, because they illustrate an essential contradiction in the distribution of attitudes.

CONSTRAINTS ON INTEGRATION

These contradictions in the distribution of attitudes are a theme that has emerged in various ways throughout our study. First, there is the task of accepting disabled people as normal, autonomous. The second is the need to respond to the physical dependency. We do well to the extent that we can do both at the same time, meeting their real and special needs without this contamination of an adult relationship with other fully functioning personalities. When we do not do so well, there is a contamination from the one to the other, and we patronize, protect, tell them what is good for them, and leave them, at the worst, damaged and accepting a lower order of existence.

What we call 'living in the community' can be seen in this context. The significance, the inner meaning, has to do with a real effort to keep the two balls, dependence and independence, in the air at the same time. It is a juggling act with many a slip. The emphasis is on making a real effort towards 'normalization'. We draw heavily on values sincerely held about the human rights which should not be eroded by the mere fact of physical disability. The Spastics Society scheme is a good example attempting to provide housing in the community scattered round a new estate. It highlights the difficulties of making the effort real in terms of its objectives.

The constraints in giving disabled people the same status as autonomous human beings that we fondly believe we give ourselves is further confused by the limitation that exists for all of us in making our way in the world that has expectations of us, some of which we either do not like or cannot meet. The physically disabled may be restricted in a number of specific ways in living their lives in the community. For example, there is the need for physical care. This may put special demands on families or neighbours, but also on the 'community' resources of help and social services. These are chronically[2] under-subscribed, and in what we might call their own specialized environments where patients or clients come to them, to their 'territories', patients and clients have to live according to professional definitions of what is realistic for them.

There is also the need for social support. The important point here is whether people feel good in themselves, or put another way, how they value themselves as people. We might usefully think of 'internal status symbols', as being more important than what is on the surface. The material evidence of success in life is only significant for what it means inside us,

---

[2] In our first draft, the audio-typist transcribed 'chronically' as 'comically'.

although we may try to objectify personal worth in terms of external achievement. Internal status is not the same as being in employment, living in one's home, having an ordinary 'consumer' existence in a market economy, but it would be difficult to deny that these things help. If we remember that it is a chronic and common condition for many disabled people to be unemployed, to live on social security, to be dependent on the bureaucracy of the welfare state – all things that we reasonably expect to be demoralizing to the able-bodied when these things happen to them – then the achievement of internal status is that much more significant. Social support in these terms is what allows people to value themselves despite being a disadvantaged group of society.

Then there is the need for 'integration'. There is no real advantage in living in the community if this is only a front for isolation and exclusive contact in a 'world of the disabled' equivalent to that found in a total institution. If community contact means only going to a day centre or being gaped at when going shopping, or even going to meetings of voluntary groups to do with the disabled – if that is *all* it means, then the individual is hardly integrated in the wider society of which he is a part.

The constraints all have to do with the contradictory virtues of seeing people as 'really normal' and at the same time offering them what is hopefully 'positive discrimination' to let them be 'normal'. Those involved can be excused for thinking that they've been going round in circles – vicious circles. The constraints are about fitting people into categories where they straddle these categories, normal and disabled, as expressed in various forms.

Perhaps the most basic example of this is to do with the structure of financial provision for the severely disabled. They need to be in institutional care but a local authority has financial responsibility for that care. Those who have been in residential care are still a responsibility of their so-called 'sponsoring authorities', though they may not have lived in the local authority's boundaries for many years. If they want to move into a new housing scheme their authorities have to agree to give this financial support, although it may cost less and certainly is guaranteed not to cost more. So already there is a major constraint on the normality of the scheme. The people moving from one place to go and live in another have to get the agreement of the local authority in a third place.

The immediate implication of this – subject to long negotiations between various interested parties including DHSS, the Department of the Environment, the local authorities, the Development Corporation of the new town in which the scheme is being introduced – is that flats set around the new housing estate ('ordinary' flats modified to meet the physical needs of those going to live there) have to be registered as 'Part 3', though the Part 3 provisions are those that affect all kinds of residential units for the disabled, as for other disadvantaged groups, *who cannot live in their own homes*.

FIRST IMPRESSIONS

So are these people not living in their own homes? Psychologically, they think they are, and their initial impressions underline the distinction between 'living in the community' and residential care.

The first residents were able to move into the new housing only after our own project should have been completed. However, we kept in touch with the scheme and were able to visit some of the residents in their new environments.

'It's like escaping out of prison.'

'I am my own boss now.'

Initial impressions – theirs and ours – were favourable. The residents – or clients: to call them residents was reminiscent of being in residential care – spoke enthusiastically of the sense of freedom and independence that they were now experiencing. One resident, invited to a conference to give his impressions, took with him his front door key and his pension book. He was now paying 'them', rather than having an allowance handed over to him. Although the flats were still Part 3 housing, the clients talked of having their own place. Psychologically if not legally, they were thinking more like tenants than clients.

There were usual times arranged for staff to come to meet their physical needs. Some had a main meal at mid-day; others in the evening. Otherwise they were left alone, unless they called on the intercom system. One client talked of loneliness and depression, and of a half-articulated idea of wanting to go back to residential care. Another missed the activities of a workshop, but would not go back – 'even if you put a bomb under me'. A man, asked if he was lonely, responded by outlining the activities of his day. He did not have time to be lonely. The clients made their own friends among each other, but they were also able to make relationships with neighbours. A man had joined a local church group, and was visiting an old man in sheltered accommodation on the estate.

The flats demonstrated varying standards of cleanliness and order. Some were almost clinical, in the manner of rooms in residential units. Others showed evidence of domesticity in action. The clients had different abilities and motivation to get out and about. One man was able to do his own gardening and had applied for an allotment. Those with electric chairs could use the paths of the new city, and some had made their own way to the city centre. Others used taxis. 'When we wanted to go shopping before, it was only possible if there were six of us wanting to go. Now we can just pick up the phone and organize it ourselves.'

THE IDEAL AND REALITY

At this stage it would be too early to evaluate such a project, but even thinking about evaluation raises the question of what would be relevant criteria for judging the success or failure of the experiment. Immediately it is inevitable that we make comparisons with the residential care from which the participants had come. But it is likely that in time such relative statements will lose their force and the project will then be judged according to criteria of 'normal' living.

The new residents are using a scarce resource; it would be irresponsible to waste it on those unable to cope emotionally with the change from orthodox institutional care, and so assessments by social workers and wardens of their present homes are taken into account. To give them a chance of making the adjustment they go to stay in specially adapted flats in a residential hostel. These assessments are primarily of their own needs but inevitably assessments are also in terms of the applicants' supposed chances of making a go of it in the new scheme. This is an aspect of what we might call the 'sense of reality' principle, and at least one applicant has not been offered a place after his stay in a hostel, because his ambitions were inconsistent with what could reasonably be expected of him living in the community.

All this may be sensible and sensitively carried out but it is certainly different from applying for an ordinary tenancy on the same estate. The disabled accept all this as their lot, however irritated they may be by a process that means that those who have applied to go to a new scheme may have been waiting two years. In making a transfer from one kind of residential unit to something organized according to the same basic economic and social structure, the important transition from living in an institution to living in the community is necessarily blurred. This is well illustrated by the problems of drafting a 'tenancy agreement'. There is always the pressure on people to be 'good citizens' and live up to our expectations of them.

On the face of it, the project is highly experimental and challenging to existing prejudices about the potential for independent living by very disabled people. The idea that those who would otherwise live in institutional care may live separately in their own homes is exciting in itself and may have wider implications of thinking about the dependency needs of disabled people.

The history of the project has shown that the idea is difficult to realize. All kinds of pressures serve to constrain this new-won freedom. The relationship with sponsoring authorities has meant that the project has to appear to provide at least the equivalent to Part 3 accommodation. In getting away from institutional care it is necessary to work within a limit of what is traditionally seen as institutional care.

There are also pressures to get the scheme to fit in with policy in the Spastics Society. The identity of the scheme links it with the Spastics Society. Ideas of including people with other handicaps are put forward but, of course, have to take second place. Those who are in the Society are the responsibility of the Society, whether they go to live at Milton Keynes or not. This puts heavy pressure on residents to be 'realistic' in terms of the provision that may be made for them. This serves to confirm institutional pressures on residents who are so used to being disabled and being dependent that their ideas of personal autonomy may well be fragile and easily eroded.

The co-ordinating committee, able-bodied representatives for the needs of the disabled, were pushing back the limits of what is thought to be realistic for them by trying to provide a different environment to meet the known needs of some people in long-term residential care. The reputation of the Spastics Society was at stake as well as the happiness of potential residents. In attempting a shift – always in balance – drawing more from the 'really normal' rather than the 'not whole' in their attitudinal set – those representing the needs of the disabled were still subject to forces that confirm existing concepts of the disabled identity. In trying something new, their own external credibility was at stake.

Management has been defined as: to provide the boundary conditions within which members of the organization manage their roles and relationships in such a way as to produce effective performance of the task (Miller 1977). Those working at the task were in this case attempting to 'understand and benefit from the apparently far-out ideas of the seeming radical' (Bolt 1972), but they simultaneously had to draw from their existing sources of authority in representing the disabled to the outside world: otherwise, like the disabled themselves, they could also be thought to be 'unrealistic'.

3
Authority and power

BACKGROUND

Following our principle of looking for live examples of the
exercise of dynamic interaction between disabled people and
their social and psychological environment, we made contact
with a new residential unit for physically disabled adults in the
London Borough of Camden. The first visit to 48 Boundary
Road was a courtesy call, part of the general process of
gathering information about recent developments in the
provision for the severely disabled. From that visit there
developed a relationship between the researcher and the staff
and residents at Boundary Road, so that it was possible to
observe them engaging with issues about the principles and
practice of care, and also to take these issues further in
discussion.

Further meetings led to the invitation from senior staff in
consultation with residents to attend a weekly staff-residents
meeting, and then to attend a weekly meeting of all staff. These
were unique opportunities to try to identify attitudes as they
were expressed, and also to look at the impact of principles on
practice. Certain factors contributed to this experience. The
head of home was appointed on his reputation as an innovator.
He had previously opened another unit, where he had successfully pursued a policy of 'open government', with residents
taking responsibility for their own actions. The building was
designed to be the best possible space for residential care. The
local authority, in commissioning the building and appointing
the Head of Home, were showing a commitment to pushing
back the boundaries of what might be considered appropriate
provision for severely disabled people needing residential care.

In the group meetings and in informal discussion, we had
the opportunity to examine with residents and staff how their

49

ideas worked out in practice, what were their aspirations and worries, and how their joint enterprise in innovation in a residential setting was stimulated or confined by their relationship with the outside world. The account that follows focuses on issues of authority and power, as these seemed to be the prevailing themes of much of the creative work in setting up the new unit. Also they are significant in our wider discussion of the distribution of attitudes. So this is only one slice of the history of this group of people as they attempted to implement a model of good practice, and is not intended to give an overall view of their achievement.

THE MEANING OF THE PHYSICAL SPACE

This unit for twenty-six physically disabled residents was sited on a new housing estate and fitted with the general appearance of white concrete and private terracing on the estate. It had no name – only a street number at the entrance, like all others on the estate. The aims were to provide a special environment for the disabled while integrating them in the community. The question of whether these aims were contradictory or supportive of each other was apparent at the planning stage of this new building, for the architects were different from those responsible for the rest of the estate. It seems that designing this unit was a specialized task but the outcome was to be a building that integrated with its surroundings.

The physical space is impressive to the eye. Two terraces of private rooms give the residents private access for whom they wish to their own rooms, while adjacent there are separate living areas for each small section of four rooms, with kitchens and toilets and bathrooms. Two lifts give access to these terraces and also the ground floor with other common facilities: a large kitchen, laundry, swimming pool, and open areas for general use. There are also flats for some of the senior staff and for volunteers on temporary placements. Inside the building the feature that seems almost to be a symbol of disabled living in a non-handicapping environment is the long ramp that sweeps down impressively to the ground floor open area.

Outside there were roof gardens, inside there was a display

of house plants. Was this emphasis on growth and flowering physical expression of the 'horticultural model' of residential care? In examining what was the philosophy of this new unit, it is possible to look at the principles that became established in the first few months about the uses made of the different parts of the building.

(a) *The living area of the residents*

There was one principle that stood out amongst all the others: where the residents lived was private to them. This meant that no one else went into this area unless they were staff working with these residents or visitors invited in by the residents. Put like that, this statement seems straightforward and reasonable, unlikely to be the subject of controversy. In fact it was a principle that was subject to much discussion among the staff and residents. Nobody disagreed with the sentiment; the question was, what did it mean in practice?

One argument went as follows: this was the residents' home and they had the same rights as any other person living at home. This analogy with ordinary housing was tenuous, even tendentious; anyway it was always being tested. For example, there was a wide interest among architects and planners in the new building: were they to be excluded? Also there was similar interest from those who worked with the disabled in other residential settings. Other disabled people who might be potential residents had a direct interest and purpose. Social workers, social work tutors and their students might want to know about the living conditions of residents, especially if the students on placement were going to work with them. All these categories add up to a lot of people, and this does not take into account council officials, fire officers, and so on, who might have official business. The concept of normal privacy was thus maintained in the face of pressure to diminish the authority of residents in controlling the boundaries around their private lives. They were not only themselves, but – like it or not – they represented others who might be like them: having the identity of being disabled means that the individual is approached not for who he is, but because he is disabled.

The layout of the building also allowed for internal testing of

51

these boundaries. On the terraces the living areas for each group of four residents led on, one from another. The convenience of passing through was such that at times both staff and residents might themselves seem only to go through the motions of being invited into a private area. This kind of disabled living was also going to be communal living, which could be good or bad. It happened that at the end of one day, four or five staff were having coffee with two residents. Had they really been invited or were they taking advantage?

The convention that people were living in their own home was confused by the fact that they were living a communal life and were subject to the dynamics of communal living. But they were there primarily because they were disabled people who needed physical care and not because they chose a communal life. So the expression of attitudes in ensuring appropriate privacy for the residents had to be understood in two ways: that they were normal people who happened to be living in a communal life, and that they were disabled people who had to accept necessary intrusion into their lives. Within the institution there was a certain amount of cultural exclusivism directed at ignorant outsiders, who would expect to be able to walk into the residents' space and so had to be educated. Outsiders were felt to have a 'not quite whole' view of the situation. Showing them up helped to reinforce an internal view the residents had of themselves, restoring their human rights as 'really normal'.

The organization of the small units was made complex by a wish to see them as self-contained and autonomous, while there were other pressures to see them as part of a whole. To what extent did staff belong to the separate sections? What happened when they helped out in other sections? Was an emotional as well as a physical attachment of staff to this or that unit[1] a sign of health in the institution or an inconvenience that had to be overcome when staff were moved?

Meetings in the small residential groups were a forum for staff and residents to plan their activities and to determine

---

[1] Later these units (consisting of four rooms plus shared facilities) became known as flats. Thus the 'ownership' of the space by the residents was symbolically taken a stage further.

priorities. They gave an opportunity for residents to take responsibility for themselves, and also for the staff to do 'social work'. The way in which the staff attached to these groups went about their tasks necessarily reflected attitudes about disability. In particular: were disabled people requiring local authority care to be thought of as clients with problems? Were the staff to be thought of as instruments of the residents' will, or as agents of the local authority with responsibilities for managing their care?

The private areas where the residents lived provided an arena within which the care relationship between staff and residents was continuously tested. To an extent this work also remained private, and while senior staff supervised those giving direct physical care there remained a certain confidentiality about what was an intimate example of social organization. Thus even within the institution there were sub-groups with their own understanding of what they were like and the public face which they showed to others.

(b) *The ground-floor area*

This area, in contrast, was seen as a public area and increasingly as an area where residents had no more rights than other users in the housing estate or further afield. The use to which the ground floor was to be put, and by whose authority, was discussed with a lot of feeling by both staff and residents and it was an issue that at times brought out into the open the potential or actual conflicts of interest between staff and residents.

The residents had their evening meal communally prepared by the cook, but was this a leftover habit from other institutional care? The architects had provided two laundries, one each for staff and residents. This was inconsistent with the philosophy: one was converted into a meeting room. A carpeted area was used for meetings and for social events. The coffee area also served as the setting for a buffet meal after the weekly group meeting.

These adjustments were internal to staff and residents. Others involved relationships with the surrounding community. The social club committee was applying for a bar

53

licence. The carpeted area was also used by a yoga group from outside. Notices advertised the coffee bar as open to all-comers during the day, and it was hoped that local people would use the facility. Part of the open space was taken over as a studio for artists and craftsmen, one a disabled man from another residential establishment. Mothers and toddlers from the neighbourhood used the swimming pool. Concerts and other entertainments were arranged by staff and widely advertised by posters in the London press. A theatre group used the space for rehearsal. Disabled self-help groups held occasional meetings there and the tenants association for the estate held its annual general meeting there. One of the senior staff was responsible for this 'community' side of the work. His aim was to make the ground floor a resource to the community and in this way the institution would not be a closed world of the disabled.

Some residents made their own links with the outside world through running an advice centre for the disabled, or employment, or attending conferences and training courses for social workers, representing the residents on the tenants' association, and so on. But the initiative was not left altogether with them. While it was accepted that they had a responsibility and freedom to run their own lives, they did not have authority to determine by their own interests or indifference what would be the public face of the institution within the local community. The head of home remained accountable to the Social Services Department.

Discussion became dispute when residents learned that one of their care staff was to be replaced by a newcomer and that he would instead go to work with senior members of staff in developing further the community activities. It was as if the two parts of the building, the private and the public, were becoming separate, and that there was a symbolic split between two sets of attitudes. Firstly, that the disabled were their own people living their own lives and using the staff to make possible their independent living; and, secondly, that they were in the care of the local authority and so part of the social services provision generally and that they should not think that the world revolved around their needs. This split allowed an outlet for staff to take initiatives on their own account; as social workers employed by the local authority, their residents were clients and part of the community.

The ground floor area was a public arena where the disabled were able to interact with others but could not expect the rules all to be to their own benefit. It was an arena which the disabled might want to control, but they would have to negotiate for what they wanted. One resident suggested that outsiders should pay for the use of their space, but otherwise it was the beginning of the end of the positive discrimination that they enjoyed upstairs. It was also an arena where the able-bodied could reassert their professional authority. It was most evident here – though also true upstairs – that the staff were management, representatives of the local authority, and accountable to the local authority.

(c) *Other areas*

The staff flats remained private. The question was at least raised whether anyone living with staff in a flat was also a resident of the building, to be invited to residents' meetings. 'Resident' in its dictionary meaning is a neutral word, but in this context implied 'disabled client in residential care' and in the end it did not make sense to revert to the neutral meaning. One staff flat became vacant and was then occupied by two disabled residents, a married couple, and in this way the area given over to residents' living was extended.

There was very little office space. The reception area was manned by a resident who applied for the job as clerical officer after that staff member left. Staff meetings were held in cramped corners, at least until the former laundry was converted. There was no staff rest room or dining room. In this way staff on duty worked always in areas where the residents were living. Finally, the roof gardens became a focus for issues about ownership. The Parks Department of the local authority had responsibility for maintaining these areas but residents also wanted to take responsibility for putting in their own plants and doing their own weeding. The gardeners had their job to do and it was not part of their job, as they saw it, to take instructions from residents.

A Life Together

This description of the home for the disabled immediately raises issues about power and authority. For attitudes reflect role relationships and these are determined to a large extent by the process of the legitimization of behaviour, of what is seen as appropriate in this or that context. Already we have seen that different areas of the building were subject to shifts of balance between the disabled residents and those who worked with them, and those from outside who had an interest in what was going on. These shifts of balance give a perspective by which to examine attitudes as expressions of power and authority. What has happened to our ideas of institutional and community care?

When we think of institutional care, there are some implicit advantages to us – that is, the wider society. We think it gives us the opportunity to give the disabled better care than they could otherwise get. It provides occupation and perhaps employment for the disabled people and also employment for those who want to work with them. More suspect, perhaps, are feelings of relief that we are doing something for them without having to change our own ways of living and so isolating those who, in a number of ways, might be disturbing to our own values. Ultimately then, there is some element of control of a problem by providing the best possible institutional care.

The advantages to them, that is the disabled, must again include the opportunity for them to get better care. This might also lead to positive aspects of structured activity – a social system. It allows them to get away from home which, even if it were possible for them to stay there, might be even more controlling and persecutory and leave them dependent in a family setting, whose dynamics would conflict with their personal growth. It also provides a communal life different from the isolation of living in the community. Additionally, there is some protection from the excesses of an acquisitive and selfish society where they are thought to get in the way.

Ideally residential care is about providing a space in which disabled people are free to realize their potential. That was the stated primary task at this local authority unit for residential care. In an organization or enterprise, those involved usually have some idea of where they fit in. Their roles in relation to the task of the organization – the production of some kind of output – give them a definite place in the hierarchy or an implicit sense of their relationship to those around them or both.

The head of home is visible, appointed by and accountable to the local authority. The head is on the boundary of the institution and represents it in the wider context of residential provision by the local authority. There is a deputy head, and senior workers, each responsible for the units of four residents and the other care staff. Other staff take housekeeping responsibilities, to do with administration, catering and cleaning, and so on. Even students and volunteers, though they have continuing accountability to the sponsoring bodies, are for the time they work there part of the straightforward system of authority delegated from above. All of these people are selected, it is assumed, on the basis of their competence to do the work.

The disabled in residential care are not part of the formal hierarchy. In fact in formal organizational terms they are invisible. In contrast to the staff, they are selected primarily on the basis of need; then there are other bases of eligibility: for example, residential qualification with the local authority or some other authority prepared to pay the necessary fee. And further, there are less easily defined criteria to do with their suitability to live in this establishment and not some other. In effect, the residents are assessed in terms of need and then acceptability. The first may look to be objective and the second a subjective judgement, but both are criteria that are in fact determined by the management, the head of home, and those beyond him in the social services hierarchy.

In this instance, at Camden, one factor in selecting residents was given a certain emphasis. The management was consciously looking at people with an eye to their potential ability to take responsibility for themselves, that is their ability to develop their sense of personal autonomy, whatever their disability and the extent of their physical dependence. An example was sometimes given to explain what we are here calling personal autonomy. A disabled man may be unable to put on his shirt. The care worker is there to do that for him. But the care worker does not choose the red or blue shirt, he asks the resident. If the answer is 'I don't mind, whichever you like', that response is unacceptable. The resident is making an unacceptable demand on the worker in asking him to choose the shirt. The worker is there only to carry out the resident's will, to put on the shirt that he has chosen. This is consistent with the management's aim in opening this new establishment – to provide a space where residents could exercise their personal autonomy both in small and great matters – and they were looking for residents who would take the best advantage of that space.

The residents at Boundary Road felt themselves to be privileged, in the sense that they believed that they were living in the best available residential unit. But this question of privilege is full of contradictions. One resident was told he was fortunate to be there. He responded acidly that there was nothing fortunate about having a progressive disease. Perhaps it was to be expected that the individual who could put this point with most feeling was only recently disabled: he retained a strong sense of his able-bodied status. Put another way, his bitter rejection of the casual well-wisher, who instinctively looks on the bright side, was open to the interpretation that he had not adjusted to his disability. To those who do not experience his sense of loss, this vision could seem paranoid. In fact, the interrelationship of loss and change as demonstrated by Marris is important to any understanding of the shifting realities of disability (Marris 1974).

The residents have, on the face of it, the opportunity to live their own lives. When they get up or go to bed, when they eat, also what they eat and where they eat it, how they occupy their time, these are everyday concerns that they may decide for themselves. In such ways, the restrictive practices of institutional life, where the individual has to obey rules made for him in the interests of all, are to a great extent removed.

There are necessarily still constraints on individual freedom, even in the most ordinary matters. Residents can only do those things for which they are dependent on the staff when staff are available to do things for them. An advantage of attaching staff to a small group of four residents is that they can sort out priorities for themselves. If a resident wants to go out for the afternoon and needs an escort, the other residents are going to have to do without their care-worker. Residents, according to this way of thinking, are taking responsibility for coping with the inevitable restrictions on them. This is different certainly from a restrictive regime, where residents, being physically dependent, are expected to conform to the regulations put out for their benefit. (There is always the suspicion, of course, that such regulations first have to undergo a sort of censorship to make sure they are also in the interests of staff.) But this concept of personal autonomy can only be taken so far. Many of the discussions in the weekly group meeting were to do with how far.

The separation of night and day had a certain significance in determining the limits of residents' autonomy and staff accountability. According to the rota, staff went off duty from eleven o'clock at night to seven-thirty in the morning. Two staff slept in: for this they received a sleeping-in allowance. This was an arrangement that residents had agreed: it allowed for more staff to be available in the day and the implication was that in general residents would not need a lot of care at night. It was not a nursing home, and the two staff would be available to cope with any emergencies. This raised the question, what is an emergency? The more liberal the stand-point, the wider the interpretation of an emergency.

There were two separate issues here. Firstly, it was increasingly a fact of life that all residents did not go to bed by eleven o'clock. No regulation insisted on an early night, and several residents regularly stayed up until midnight or beyond. As it happened one resident was now requiring a certain amount of care at night and he had to be turned in his bed at 1.30 a.m. The staff who were sleeping in did not attempt to go to bed before that time and often they were working continuously from 11 to 1.30 in putting people to bed.

The second issue was that they might then be woken four or five times during the night by emergency calls. What, in this context, was an emergency? One of the residents called the sleeping-in staff to light his cigarette: this was thought by some staff to be justified; for the resident was not able to sleep, he was a smoker, and his lighter was broken. Many calls were because people were not comfortable, and that was also sufficient reason to call for assistance: you don't lie there in discomfort for hours

59

because you are reluctant to make demands on the staff.

There was little pressure from the immediate care-staff to force residents to be 'realistic' about going to bed at night. No one with a physical relationship of caring wanted to tell a resident that he had to fit in with what care-staff wanted. This applied particularly to newcomers enjoying their new-found freedom: a married couple were living it up, and there was a question whether they were doing so out of the euphoria of coming together from separate residential units before, or whether it was to be their pattern of life anyway. They tended to stay up late, and on one occasion at two o'clock the woman was getting her hair washed by one of the staff. (This is one example of a call on staff at night that was thought by the staff group to be unnecessary.) Further discussion led to the suggestion that if three residents wanted to stay up late they could get into their nightclothes when appropriate, so that whoever put them into bed at last would not have to go through the routine of undressing and ablutions. That was appealing to the staff, but immediately they worried that a 'rule' was emerging – all residents must be in their nightclothes by eleven o'clock.

Because the staff were sensitive to such issues, they could also feel the pressures to make rules. A senior member of staff argued that they should not persecute those who stayed up late, and not interfere unless they were being very demanding, for they were, in compensation, less demanding from nine-thirty to eleven o'clock, allowing staff time for other residents. In discussion the suggestion was made that staff even in some ways encouraged the residents to stay up late. The staff who went off duty at eleven o'clock sometimes found it difficult just to go off into the night and so they might tend to delay in the residents' area.

The work load on staff who were sleeping in was a problem: if the residents did not call them at night, they could still have the full complement of staff during the day, but if the demand at night continued it might become necessary to introduce a night shift, and reduce the complement of day staff.

As it was, the situation made a sharp distinction between the needs of residents at day and during the night. With staff sleeping in, the residents had to judge what was reasonable as an emergency. One resident might want to come home from a party at 4 a.m. Was this acceptable? Answer – yes . . . but not often. At the same time the staff were having to make an adjustment in their relationship to the residents: they were not there to do anything they might want. But, as we have seen from the examples discussed, the staff were interpreting an emergency liberally – in the spirit of their day-time ethic. As residents found it difficult to stop being autonomous human beings at eleven o'clock, so staff found it difficult to require the residents to forgo their own real needs so that they could rest between their waking shifts.

Here then was the expression of an inevitable conflict of interest between the disabled and their carers. But it also shows that maintaining a balance, a reasonable resolution of the conflict with mutual respect for the other's needs, was subject to contrary forces – that the disabled were having to check again their perceptions of themselves as having ordinary needs (a late night out, or a smoke), and the carers were likewise exploring the realistic limits of their care. So the disabled were drawing again on a model of care that saw their dependent needs as subservient to meeting the needs of the able-bodied, while the carers were likewise holding off what they feared were unrealistic demands of the disabled.

The significant point in these discussions was that when any one standpoint was taken it was clearly in contra-distinction to another standpoint. For example, it was made evident in these discussions that residents were responsible for the management of their own health. This did not stop at their handling their own medication, which itself turned into a debate about the responsibility between the disabled and staff in residential care. On occasions, staff expressed concern about the symptoms they had observed or that residents had told them about. But the principle was clear. Residents were in their right minds so they could decide if and when they wanted to see a doctor. The staff were not therefore to take the initiative away from the residents by deciding to call a doctor. Within the culture of the unit this principle was favourably compared with the practice in other places of having a resident nurse or nurses and doctors making regular visits. Some of the residents had come from establishments run by nurses and they reinforced the antipathy felt towards what was thought of as a false model for seeing disabled as patients.

The distinction between a nursing or medical model, as understood in this setting, and a social work model meant that at least one staff experienced a confusion of role identity. She was a care-worker but she had nursing qualifications. She came into the job to get away from nursing. The trouble was that she was used informally by staff and residents as a nursing resource. A female resident consulted her and was reassured about minor symptoms. A care-worker noticed dry skin on the head of a resident – he was combing his hair – and asked the nurse if it was serious. She was ill at ease. Firstly, as a nurse she was not trained to diagnose, and certainly not without seeing the 'patient'. Secondly, she did not want the role of 'nurse' and the resident was not her patient. In this she was supported by the head of home: the residents could call on outside medical care as they needed it. (Or was this precluding the disabled residents from the sort of informal advice that the able-bodied get from friends and neighbours?)

The only nursing that these staff were expected to do was the kind of activity that an able-bodied or partially disabled person might otherwise do for himself in the way that, say, a diabetic injects himself with insulin. But we can see, as Illich has said, how easily healing ceases to be the activity of the individual in relation to himself and becomes instead the duty of the physician (Illich 1974).

This was a unit managed by a social services department and it was possible to castigate the health service ('good at cure but lousy at care') from a social services stand-point. The question then was whether staff imposed their social-work view of the world on residents in a way similar to that complained of about nursing staff and doctors. The management, both the senior and junior staff, questioned their caring role as residential workers and the limits they wanted to put on this role in seeking to influence the lives of the residents/clients. To the extent that they believed that disabled people were normal people with disabilities, they liked the residents to show off their normality by being stable, ambitious, purposeful – supra-normal! The status of normality was useful as a way of fending off accusations of abnormality – and 'No one is normal' is an effective disclaimer of any deviance.

Some residents were more obviously clients with problems and the task with them – helping them to overcome their own failure to realize their potential – involved the care staff in making judgements about that potential. The ambivalence of the relationship was expressed in the concern that staff felt about issues of confidentiality. A resident might talk to a care-worker. Was that as a confidant, a kind of friend, or as a social worker whose report would later be discussed with senior staff? If a worker was available to the resident to give him physical help when he wanted it, it could seem exploitative to use his physical dependence as a way of getting to his 'problems' – even if he was not asking for that kind of help. The disabled individual in this setting is thus living up (or down) to the expectations of the staff. If he seems to be coping he reinforces their idea of the disabled as normal. If he is having difficulties he confirms them in their helping role where they can take more initiative than is possible for them in the carrying out of physical tasks under his direction.

This is an example of the contradictory but complementary attitudes that we have seen in different contexts. The disabled are applauded when the able-bodied are able to admire their efforts according to their own standards, and made psychologically as well as physically dependent when they fail to meet our requirements of them as 'good citizens'.

CONFLICT AND THE CARE RELATIONSHIP

By following the discussions of groups of residents and staff, we saw the care relationship explored for its potential in meeting the needs of those in residential care. The care relationship provides a context, in which attitudes are expressions of in-group and out-group membership and individuals identify with, but are separate from, those with whom they have intimate relationships to do with physical care and dependency. There is conflict because the two people in the relationship have overlapping functions that might 'normally' be combined and belong to a single individual. So they are attempting a single action but with two personal constructs of the meaning of this action. The two constructs can never be identical. It is a bit like running a three-legged race. You can do it and do it well but no one can pretend that it is the same as or as effective as normal running.

The helper has two roles; a dependent role that takes its lead from the disabled person and an independent role that belongs to the helper. A good demonstration of the two roles together may be observed in the feeding of someone who is unable to feed himself. The helper puts the food on the fork and puts the fork into the other's mouth. The other may give instructions about what should be on the fork but in general an experienced helper is able automatically to feed someone in this way. At the same time, the helper may be feeding himself. The helper tries to combine his independent and dependent roles. One worker observed how he left the same kind of food at the side of his plate and on the plate of the disabled person.

Where the needs of the helper and those of the disabled person are not in conflict there is no problem. Where these needs are in conflict something has to give. It is not surprising therefore that a ready indication of a 'good' attitude towards care is that the disabled person has a high level of autonomy in controlling his life through the medium of those helping him. Choosing when you get up and go to bed, when you eat, what you eat, and the way you eat it – these are, one might think, simple things to get right, and yet they are so important to the individual that they are the most ready examples given of what people were looking for when they hoped for a better care system. For such basic freedoms it seems it is necessary to move heaven and earth.

Why should such a simple thing be so important? It requires a radical shift in the way that we think about the disabled. In psychological terms it is a shift from projection of inadequacy on to the cripple to identification with his needs – an identification out of sympathy or empathy – arising from our own feelings of internal disadvantage and disarray. According to one model, they are disabled and have to make the best of it and fit into the world. To the extent that they protest, they are thought to be further handicapped, maladjusted in some way, in addition to other physical disabilities. In this context, the disabled develop skills in meeting the needs of those on whom they are dependent. They feel or feign gratitude and try not to be too much bother.

The emphasis on practical aspects of disabled living is necessary as long as there are practical problems that could be solved, but in a way the continuing importance of matters of access, regimented routines, and other evidence of second-hand citizenship is indicative of the basic level of the debate at the moment. Until these things have been sorted out and the reason for the slow progress exposed, any further questioning about the emotional quality of life of disabled people is necessarily difficult to check against reality. This reality, that disabled people have choices in their lives and with help can have autonomous personalities, separate from the person-alities of those on whom they are physically dependent, has not yet been fully realized.

But the two levels, practical freedom of choice and the emotional quality of life, are linked at every stage. For example, the disabled person, if freed of external constraints on the course of action (such as his social worker not thinking it realistic or the care staff thinking he is being 'demanding'), is then faced with his real disability. The question is now whether he really wants to and really can carry out this course of action. Perhaps for the first time he feels the force of his own disability rather than the disabling constraints of a 'protective' environ-ment. Before he gets to this stage he is caught up in negotiations with others, where he is expected, maybe, to be courageous (in the eyes of others) but certainly sensitive to the needs of others, grateful, and accepting of the social space made for him. That the residents were able to control their own lives would be an indication of success of this new unit. But if they then chose to be passive, to do nothing, and were self-absorbed and apathetic, turning their backs on the outside world, this would not look like the kind of success that the management had in mind.

So residents and staff in the new residential unit explored how care may compensate for the lack of physical function of the residents on their own, and thereby realize their potential as human beings. The head of home gave a threefold definition of task; the first task he suggested was a 'social work' task with the residents, helping them to come to terms with their disability. Secondly, there was the community work that was to be done, in relating the residential unit to the larger world outside. The third task was physical care; but it only became the first priority if it was not being done right.

The staff have been described as 'extensions' to the residents. This may be overstating the case but the basis of care is thereby assumed to be dictated by the needs of the residents. When this point of view was put forward at a conference for professional workers, it raised understandable anxiety in those working in other residential care settings. It was interpreted as a takeover, a putsch by the residents, a short-lived revolution that could not be tolerated for long by staff. The point was put that staff also have needs and exist in their own right.

At the conference, we asked someone in a wheelchair whether it was important to be polite to staff, always to say thank you for anything done, and were told that you had to keep in with those caring for you because you are dependent on them. At the residential unit, the staff group discussed from their point of view whether it was necessary to like residents or not. Some said that it did not make a difference or should not make a difference to the quality of care, but there was some sense of the importance of identification in carrying out effectively their task in a care relationship. This left unresolved how far liking or disliking is related to the role that one takes in relation to another person; if staff are working well they like the residents in the work setting, though they might not like them as friends outside that setting.

The question of whether one had to like the other raised further issues about the role. Was it simply to provide physical care? Perhaps liking or not liking was not important then. But if one had an implicit social work role – that is, providing most, if not all, of the social contact that residents had – then liking and disliking did become important.

Other issues, discussed in theoretical terms by staff and residents alike, also demonstrated the concern of residents to explore the boundaries of their right to self-determination. These issues concern the possibility of residents getting into deviant behaviour – the taking of social drugs like cannabis was mentioned. The management was unequivocal that it could not knowingly tolerate illegal activity in local authority premises. What then of the principle that staff were there to give physical aid to the residents in accordance with their wishes? In this case, it might mean rolling a joint. Necessarily, staff were in a position of censoring the residents' actions. One result of being disabled, it seems, is that it is difficult to break the law. Similar issues were rehearsed with reference to suicide. In this case it was agreed that a resident was not free to ask a care-worker to help him in taking his own life as this would have serious consequences for the worker. (The question whether a worker doing an illegal act in assisting a resident to carry out an illegal act should be accused with the resident was answered pragmatically, that the resident would need the careworker during his prison sentence anyway!)

These discussions were thus often joking and good humoured, but their serious intent was never in doubt. The disabled and the able-bodied alike were probing what was the reality behind their ideal of autonomous living by the residents. The contradictions of being free within the constraints of what others are prepared to do for you, were worked out in a number of scenarios with different protagonists. Thus, when a resident was cautious about his rights, he was told he could do what he liked. But when a resident put forward a minority view, he was likely to be corrected according to the 'philosophy'. If a resident complained, say about fire risk, he might be encouraged to challenge the authorities directly by contacting the appropriate officers. But a resident who regretted that there were delays in getting new staff was told firmly that the ratio of staff to residents was already very good compared to other establishments, and was so discouraged from complaining. The disabled role emerged from the discussions as complex and disoriented, because of the conflicting expectations of the disabled as clients and as autonomous personalities in their own right.

The residents took some personal authority for their actions; that much is clear. To the extent that they lived their lives differently, this was according to their own wishes, but it is less clear how far they exercised authority in their own right and how far they were allowed this relative freedom through the benign authority of the head of home and his employers – which might be withdrawn by a less benign successor.

What if a resident suffers an accident through the exercise of his freedom? Who would then be accountable and what would happen then? We were told an anecdote that makes the point. A disabled man lived in a residential unit for many years. In addition to other disabilities he suffered epileptic fits but wished to do things for himself, like taking a bath. It was a risk he accepted and the risk was far outweighed by his wish for privacy. But he had a fit while taking his bath and drowned. At the inquest, the coroner was critical of the residential care. He might have been more critical but it happened that the bathroom did not have proper doors, only a curtain. The dead man's wish for privacy had never been fully met and what from one point of view was an inadequacy of the establishment had saved it, and the head of home, from stronger criticism at this time of crisis.

One of the disadvantages of being disadvantaged is that you are not held responsible. This is a wider issue than that of the disabled. Take a different example. A baby is battered and social services are held to be responsible. This may be a relief to the parents who are unable to cope and do the battering, but their diminished responsibility forces social services departments into contortions of effort to fulfil their obligations to avoid instances of child abuse. The disabled, certainly those in residential care, are also people for whom the social services are held to be accountable in all respects. It is as if being disabled and in need of one kind of help they are assumed also to be inadequate and to have diminished responsibility. They also have to be saved from themselves.

The assumption of inadequacy was not part of the philosophy of the new residential unit. But the issue of accountability was not so easily done away with. In that benign environment, residents and staff were still having to relate in the wider context to what happens when some people are given a disadvantaged status, so that some advantages are then made available – including the employment of others to help them.

ACCOUNTABILITY AS A DEFENCE AGAINST FANTASY

The diminishing of personal authority is itself disabling. We can ask further what the issue of accountability tells us about attitudes. The conference for workers with the disabled, which we have mentioned, heard a talk from one of the first residents of the new unit. She described the relief that she felt in moving there after spending all her adult life in another setting where she felt she was subject to rules and regimentation. She explained how the staff on the new unit were working to fulfil her needs and to carry out her wishes as far as possible to give her some freedom of action – the same as that of an able-bodied person.

The reaction of the professional audience was, to judge by their comments, to be frightened. They soon decided that staff would not tolerate such autocratic behaviour from a resident. She had not explained that she was only fitting in with the philosophy of the unit, as she understood it, nor that the philosophy was a concept developed by the management. Furthermore, the audience speculated about what would happen if their disabled residents had such freedom of action. It seemed from their comments that two things would follow. The residents would make the lives of staff intolerable or they would kill themselves. Left to themselves the disabled would destroy us or themselves. This is an underlying assumption that helps to explain how the issue of authority reinforces those who work with the disabled from a position of enlightened guardianship.

Such a position is easily justified by reference to the emotional immaturity of this person or the preoccupation with self of another, or the overdemanding dependent behaviour of yet another. We may even agree that people are being disabled by a crippling environment. They have slowly come to accept as theirs, certain limitations that others have assumed were theirs all the time. The failures of professional care in the past – institutionalism, for example – help to keep the professional carers of today in business. Certainly this now helps the workers at Camden in defining their task, i.e. getting away from the bad old practices.

Furthermore, the idea of the accountability of the worker, retaining responsibility for the disabled in order to make good the errors of the past – individually, professionally, culturally – allows the worker to retain a sense of worth, even when he may have been failing. While the accountability stays it is still possible to assuage guilt about the fate of the disabled – one can go on doing one's best: give that up, and there is nothing, theoretically or practically, to be done. From the worker's point of view, it may seem better to keep to one's own standards of professional care, however limited, than to feel impotent to help. At least he is doing his job – the limitations are in the work, and not in himself.

THE LIBERAL POSITION

In the new residential unit, the staff at different levels expressed and held in common an affirmation that they were doing better for residents than other establishments, including those from which these residents had come. The residents were expected to confirm this belief. Newly arrived residents were told in glowing terms about their new life and they talked about the culture shock as they adapted to the freedom they were now experiencing. Their statements were received without fuss; these reactions were only to be expected. But the comparisons were taken to the extreme, with reference to establishments where residents were put to bed at four o'clock to relieve pressure on the staff.

The need to see themselves as good and others as bad was illustrated well in a staff meeting with a suggestion that a journalist might write about this establishment and about an ageing institution representing what they were trying to get away from. The making of comparisons might be valid. It is after all often a researcher's task to evaluate different systems of care. But the question here is why the staff needed to make comparisons and to keep on doing it. It was not enough for them that they were doing a good job as they saw it. It seemed that they needed to reinforce their own sense of their own right approach – allowing the authority of residents – by repeated reminders of what was wrong elsewhere – restrictions on residents. In reverse, those who worked in other settings counter-attacked with moralistic fantasies about the new unit, in particular about its 'immoral' high costs and fees.

In each case, the need is not purely defensive, i.e. countering a possible threatening attack that one is not as good as ideally one would like. The staff in the new unit were taking up a position analogous of that of the white liberal in a country practising apartheid. The liberal position in this context has been well described by Donald Woods, following his exile from South Africa (Woods 1978). There is an identification with the underdog and a wish to challenge the injustices of a society which on his behalf is maintaining the disadvantaged in a dependent and restricted environment; also an ambition to represent the interests of the disadvantaged (the disabled) by using one's influence as a better off (able-bodied) member of society.

The motivation of many staff in this new unit for the disabled was to show that residential care was not a form of apartheid or social death. They were insisting on a respect for the disabled residents as equal members of society and so attempting to expose prejudice where it occurred and to campaign, if necessary, on behalf of the disabled to work towards a different kind of society, where people would be accepted for what they were, where their abilities would be recognized and they would not be known only for their disabilities.

A summary of the liberal position indicates how authority and power get mixed up with the exercise of leadership. The new residential unit was not only going to be a good place for its residents to live in but it was to be an example to others. It was going to challenge the accepted standard in residential care. This taking up of a leadership position involved everyone who had any responsibility towards the new unit. The local authority and its social services department would expect a return on its investment going beyond the immediate provision of care. The fact of making provision for 26 disabled people was important but so was the hope of providing the best possible care for disabled people generally (not all the new residents were the statutory responsibility of that local authority but were 'imported' from elsewhere). The management of the home could be seen as providing a boundary where the residents would be protected from the worst excesses of social values emphasizing productivity and conventional status. But the weakness of the liberal's position is that ultimately the able-bodied retain authority for defining the reality within which the disabled are free to live. The new residential unit provides a model of what may be achieved in a residential setting, i.e. benign management. But its success also gives intimations of a further development of the taking of authority by disabled people themselves and, it follows, the taking of leadership in making possible innovations in their own care. This is the 'disabled power' position, an emergent force in the distribution of attitudes around disabled people.

4

Integration – the world of the disabled

ASPECTS OF LIVING IN THE COMMUNITY

Most disabled people live in their own homes. In a rough-and-ready definition of that term they are *living in the community*. In the two previous sections we have looked at the world of the disabled by identifying two residential groups in their relationship to helping agencies, a voluntary body and a local authority. We were also able to make contact with a range of people, some severely disabled, who were living in ordinary housing adapted to their needs. In this section we want to examine their relationships to their environment, and see how informally there may be a *world of the disabled* within which people attempt to manage their *disabled identity* and so come to terms with an apparently able-bodied world. We develop further the theme that disabled people have to negotiate a norm, by which they may be found acceptable by a wider society.

LIVING IN THE COMMUNITY – SUCCESS AND FAILURE

On the face of it, living in the community is easily contrasted with institutional care. The distinction is not so clear-cut in reality. Negative characteristics of institutional care – the supposed social isolation, lack of personal autonomy, lack of differentiation in aspects of one's life – may be experienced by those living in their own homes. At the same time, as our own research has shown, institutional care may not be as exclusive and limiting as is sometimes assumed (Dartington 1979). In looking now at the distribution of attitudes around disabled people living in their own homes we can see how they are subject to similar constraints as those in residential care and how they are likewise subject to the psychological projections of the able-bodied.

In our work with the disabled and those around them we

73

were made aware that individuals were thought well of or not according to unacknowledged criteria of success and failure. An explanation of this would be that their very existence as disabled people living at home is seen as a challenge. The greater the disability, the greater the challenge. More obviously even than those who are 'contained' through the circumstances of the provision of care, they are typically seen as triumphing against the odds – or failing.

So the issues facing the disabled at home are, we suggest, not very different from those in residential care. In a similar way they have to seem to be 'special' in order to achieve normal status. Again they are put to the test. The projections of the able-bodied suggest they must either succeed or fail. By their dependency they can make the able-bodied feel useful; by their independence they can serve as living demonstrations that partial damage does not have to lead to total annihilation. The fantasy that it does so lead seems deepseated. They are seen to fail when the able-bodied are unable to use them – use them either as dependency objects or, by a process of projective identification, as an inspiration in the struggle to achieve what Storr calls an integration of the personality (Storr 1970). The individual seeks in the other a model for the solution of his own problems. The interpersonal relationships of the disabled to their environment can then be seen in terms of the intrapersonal concerns of the able-bodied as well as of the disabled.

The contradictory demands that the able-bodied make of the disabled may also mean, as following examples show, that the test of success and failure is not a constant for the disabled person but requires a continuous re-adjustment of his relationship to different norms of acceptability. The success or failure of the disabled derives in part from a pretence of their ordinariness. We can see this by looking at an example of a 'success'.

Mr Hines is a self-employed accountant, married and living in his own home. He contracted polio when he was 5. His education was interrupted because the grammar school did not have access for a pupil in a wheelchair. After private tuition he was admitted to another school and so was able to continue his education so that he was accepted, on leaving school, into an accountant's office. He got his accountancy qualifications but not promotion. He thinks that his employers saw him as dependent on them and that he surprised them by leaving the job. He is now working successfully on his own with help from his wife, also disabled. They met through an organization working for the disabled – that is, through a common interest; as he put it, like the Young Conservatives.

Mr Hines' professional success has not been without its special challenges. For example, he said, it is very difficult to get the Inspector of Taxes out of his high office. Having achieved that, though, he was himself at an advantage having got the man out of his territory and on to his own level!

In such ways he is successful in his professional milieu both at work and in his social life and his disabled identity is not in conflict with his social status. Certainly he keeps his distance from any non-coping stigma attached to the world of the disabled. He keeps out of local voluntary work as much as he can, as he sees small voluntary organizations as inefficient and disorganized. At the same time he has worked as treasurer of national voluntary organizations and has been involved in major campaigns on behalf of the disabled. Even so, at an important meeting held in a prestigious London bank head-quarters, he found that the toilet for the disabled was wrongly designed. In his own home he is still, as he puts it, fighting the bureaucracy about installation of a bath hoist, and he has not held back from writing directly to the Minister of the Disabled.

Mr Hines was suggested to us as someone whom we should interview because he was a success. In his own terms also he has made a success of his life. His disability has not constrained him from living a life that was consistent with his personality and personal ambition. His involvement with the world of the disabled was also consistent with his life style.

But success can turn into a failure: those working to achieve the rehabilitation of someone disabled would like to see his integration in their own terms. Mr Watkins is paraplegic as a result of a car accident; married, with a son. A year after the accident, he was able to return from Stoke Mandeville Hospital to his own home. During that time, his wife was supportive to him and a local voluntary group was in turn involved in helping her with transport and other support. His return to his own home was itself a triumph; it allowed him to slip back into the important social network of his family and friends. The Social Services Department also took up the challenge and with the Housing Department, converted a nearby shop and upper storey into a home that was both convenient and attractive for the Watkins family. They themselves were very pleased with the new house and, again with the help of friends, decorated and furnished it to their liking.

Mr Watkins had worked in the tough male world of the docks. His aggressive personality was a source of strength in his fight to achieve his rehabilitation as someone confined to a wheelchair. He had won battles against the nursing regime at Stoke Mandeville Hospital. He uttered threats against anyone who might have ideas of interfering with his wife. While he had bouts of depression, he was determined, with his wife's support, that he had to keep going. The stress on the wife was very great and at one time she was admitted to a psychiatric hospital. Mr Watkins was able to 'rescue' her – as he told the story, he barred the doctor's way with his wheelchair while she was taken by a friend to a waiting car. This was an instance where he was still able to assert his potency and physical strength; his natural assertiveness seemed unaffected by his changed circumstances. He was ambitious for his son, encouraging his interest in boxing. He was ambitious also for the future, looking forward to the time when the compensation money came through and he would be able to provide a good life for his family. His aggressiveness was associated with a sense of humour so that he could easily mock the ill-informed reactions of the able-bodied to his disability. He was visited by an official of the DHSS. He claimed to have made the man physically sick by his description of the intimate details of his physical care – this was in answer to an incautious question as to whether he might not be able to go to work.

Mr Watkins seemed to be in a good position to negotiate a positive disabled identity. He liked to do normal things and see how others reacted. He was welcome at his local pub. He noticed that holding hands with his wife in public caused strangers to stare. He seemed fiercely independent and resistant to suggestions that, for example, he might go to a Social Services day centre.

He had the working man's suspicion of volunteers who claim to do something for nothing. However, he became involved with the local voluntary group who helped him and he wrote their newsletter. Like Mr Hines, his independence seemed to be allowing him to live a life compatible with his own values and way of looking at the world. His obvious courage – he was described as 'Mr Courage' in a local newspaper – ensured that others, both in the statutory and the voluntary sector, did their best for him. His home was a showhouse for demonstrating what could be achieved, so that this severely disabled man returned to and survived in his old environment.

But it did not work out as straightforwardly as this account might imply. Mr Watkins' aggressive stance came to be seen by some of those around him as an unrealistic non-acceptance of his disabled status; so he came to be seen as demanding and insensitive, as putting unfair pressure on his wife and child. From being 'Mr Courage' he was making a subtle transition to becoming 'difficult'. In meeting one aspect of an able-bodied idea of rehabilitation – 'standing on his own feet' – he was failing in another aspect – accepting his disability.

This example illustrates the narrowness of the line between success and failure, as determined by the perceptions of others. What is thought of as appropriate behaviour in individual circumstances can be quite narrowly defined so that it becomes necessary to walk a tightrope in avoiding the dangers of passive self-pity and acceptance of dependency or, like Mr Watkins, being seen as recalcitrant and unrealistic in maintaining psychological links with his former able-bodied life. He was still sufficiently like his able-bodied self; it was difficult for others to continue to see him indefinitely in his assumed role as good citizen, a model example, and inspiration to others.

Some people take on a deviant role when they are thought to be making an exhibition of their disability. Mr Hines referred to such a deviant: a disabled man in financial difficulty, his wife having left him, was the subject of a newspaper article. His photograph showed him in shorts – what Mr Hines called his underwear, which revealed his deformed legs – and he was thought to embarrass others by the exploitation of his physical appearance. He was somehow letting down the side and giving disability a bad name.

A Life Together

The success of disabled people in living independent lives is admired: here is evidence that people can survive damage and the unconscious fantasy that disruptive attacks are being made on them. But their success brings its own problems. If they are truly independent, this undermines their psychological usefulness as objects of able-bodied pity and sympathy (sym-pathy: suffering with – the disabled have to appear to suffer if the able-bodied are to be able to care). The man who was seen as deviant had made his suffering too obvious: his exposure of twisted limbs was threatening. If we cannot feel sympathy, we feel persecuted by the suffering of others.

In contrast, in the following example, the disabled person who makes light of disability may be seen as ungrateful – as if an attack is being made on others' sympathy. Miss Wogan, herself a paraplegic in a wheelchair, was very determined to live her own life. Like Mr Watkins, she said she did not feel disabled; she talked of the inspiration she got from Stoke Mandeville Hospital where any self-pity she might have had was taken out of her – she was shown the other patients and told that that was what she was to be like and so she had better get used to the idea. She was actively involved with the voluntary group; she liked music and dancing; she wrote an article for a local newspaper and put forward a strong argument that the disabled have the same interests and enthusiasms in life as able-bodied people. This article was strongly criticized by a worker in a day centre; he thought that Miss Wogan's approach was unrepresentative of other disabled people and gave a false impression of their dependency needs.

This comment seems, like Mr Hines' remarks about deviant behaviour, to imply a fantasized group-membership that the able-bodied thrust on the disabled – a sort of uniform made in only one size. Each disabled person is then somehow perceived by the able-bodied as speaking as a representative of 'the disabled' – notwithstanding the obvious differences between the individuals and different kinds of disabilities.

DISABILITY AND THE FAMILY

The worker might have been thinking of Mrs Bean who attended the day centre. She was very depressed and felt that she was lacking support in coping with very real problems in her life. After the amputation of a leg she found it difficult, almost impossible, to walk unaided. She moved with sticks or walked with a walking-frame and this severely limited her mobility. Recently widowed, she lived with her youngest child, now in late adolescence. She felt trapped in her home, a ground-floor flat; she recently made one expedition to a shopping centre with a married daughter but she said that she would never do it again. Her family were caring but did not seem to know how to care; they had been frustrated by her slowness and did not notice the difficulty that she had, say, with a simple task like making a bed. She felt that she was under attack from others – that they had the idea that it was her fault, that she was not properly trying – and in turn, she was critical and hostile towards those who were professionally responsible for her care, especially her GP whom she accused of failing to make an appointment at the hospital.

The depression and frustration experienced by Mrs Bean seem to leave her isolated. One can feel sorry for her but it is difficult to know how to care for her. At times she feels panicky. She finds it difficult to sleep because of the pain she is in. When he finds her crying, her son responds with 'not again, Mum'. She has to look to her family for care while her son is still looking to her to be his mother.

A close relationship within the family can sometimes seem to offer a custodial model of care, or self-care, among those living in the community, not so different from those examples of custodial care that are thought to be the defects of an insti-tution. It is remarkable how physical care can be disruptive of commonly held assumptions about family life. (And yet often staff in an institution talk of it being like a family!)

For the disabled at home, much of the physical care, of course, is done not by paid workers but by other members of the family – or friends. Mr French had the advantage that his wife was a trained nurse. He suffered from a progressive disease that left him very dependent and housebound for most of the time. He had difficulty speaking. When interviewed he left most of the answering of questions to his wife. She acted not as interpreter simply but as spokesperson so that it was impossible to tell what were his thoughts as a disabled person and what were hers as the carer. For example, she seemed to hold on to some hope of a miraculous cure. The doctor was only a telephone call away and as soon as he had news of a new treatment the telephone would ring. This hope – stated baldly – could have been the despairing defence of a dying man or the occupational defence of the professional nurse. As she spoke for him, it was impossible to tell which it was. Also her taking up this role could have been an exaggeration, or complication, of a dynamic that was already there in the marriage, before her husband became disabled. Mr French had been active in public life; now the effectiveness of his wife's care meant that there was little need for him to leave his own room. He had been articulate, but now he left her to speak for him. The impact of his disability on others was diffused through the wife who was able-bodied. She represented him with able-bodied vigour, and so to others, he seemed to be 'all right'.

Thus the family model of care can often be seen to be a prototype of the protectiveness of able-bodied representation of the needs of the disabled. It works like an inner core of the 'world of the disabled', where disability is accepted as a norm (though Mrs Bean was not, it seems, so protected): a protective boundary may distinguish this world from a wider society, where the individual might be thought to be abnormal and unable to cope.

Mr Rossiter lived in a poverty-stricken household in a depressed area of London. He was housebound in his council flat and his wife did not risk trying to take him out. Like Mr Watkins he was a man of independent spirit – and so got into great rages. He would have nothing to do with social workers. He fought his own battles, although he did not always win. He had frequently been hospitalized during the previous two years. He was waiting to be assessed by a Medical Officer from the DHSS. He was puzzled and angry that the doctors who treated him at the hospital could not sign a form to confirm his evident disability and that he had to be separately assessed.

He was determined not to go back to hospital but a combination of his obduracy and bureaucratic caution left him reliant on the resources of his family who were in every way impoverished. Mrs Rossiter accepted the main burden of care; the worst of it for her, she confided on the doorstep, was wiping his bottom. This was an intimate act that was nevertheless, in her eyes, inappropriate between husband and wife.

In both cases, Mr French and Mr Rossiter, the man became disabled in middle age and the wife responded to the changed relationship. The family adapts in attempting to provide the caring environment required by the disabled member, but as was seen it can look like a closed system, with the family locked into its internal resources in order to contain any sense of difference within the family; in its external relations the family remains an independent unit. There are two forces working to this end: because there is a family, they are able to be more independent of external services than might be possible for the disabled individual living alone; and since as a family they seem to be able to cope, the helping agencies tend reactively to assume the family's ability to cope.

One of the advantages of a 'Crossroads' care attendant scheme is that it helps to support such a closed family system of care. Professional carers, the social worker, the health visitor, the doctor, give of their time and skill, but from a standpoint outside the family. For all their effectiveness, they are making brief interventions – what Kushlick would call direct care, limited to hours or minutes (Kushlick 1975) – introducing resources and expertise from outside. Care attendants are instructed to do what the family, especially the disabled member, wants of them. This principle, essential to the success of the scheme, acknowledges the personal authority of the disabled in determining their own need – within the bonds of the family system of care. (It is the same principle in community care that we saw in residential care in Chapter 3.)

We saw the setting up of such a care attendant project. The challenge, it seemed, was not so much the recruiting of suitable care attendants, but obtaining suitable referrals from existing care agencies. There was some scepticism – from, for example, health visitors – as to whether untrained workers would be able to cope with their patients. Their professional attitude towards the disabled people, whom they visited in their homes, led them to focus on specific physical problems, which required their skills, and not to recognize so readily other aspects of the relationship of disabled people to those around them.

A Life Together

Where two disabled people marry there is theoretically and often practically mutual aid so that together they may live together more independently than either could do separately. Mr and Mrs Leyland are both cerebral palsied. They live in their own home and have a 4-year-old child. They own their car: Mr Leyland has passed the advanced driving test. They are able to live independently, having won battles to get the adaptation that they needed, for example a split-level cooker for Mrs Leyland. They have the services of a home-help. Mrs Leyland describes herself as demanding and their home-help is not as efficient as she would be if she could have done it herself. Although they are not able to get employment they feel themselves to be integrated with their community – Mrs Leyland babysits for the next-door neighbours and in doing this she has had to overcome her own negative attitude, as she sees it, about whether she could cope in an emergency. As for patronizing attitudes, they see these more in older disabled people than in the able-bodied.

Although such an example fits with the 'favourable' impression of the disabled as 'really normal', those achieving such independent status may have had to overcome the protective obstacles put in their way by able-bodied who think of them as non-coping. Another married couple, Mr and Mrs O'Leary met when they were both in residential care. They found their friendship was discouraged by the staff there and he was sent off on a course aimed to aid his 'rehabilitation' – but apparently designed to separate them!

Disabled families – where both parties are disabled – are almost, by definition, a 'success'. Just by being there they are seen to have achieved the desired integration in the community. At the same time this integration has certain characteristics. For example, their close friends tend to be associated with the world of the disabled – people they have met through voluntary organizations or through welfare rights work. In one instance, the home-help was stated to be a 'best friend'.

Stages in the integration of the disabled are achieved often through a difficult selection process, analogous to having a career – with some of the characteristics of a work career. Getting to live in one's own home is rather like promotion from residential care; instead of the key to the executive washroom you get the key to your own front door. (This is consistent with the assumptions behind the community care scheme described in Chapter 2.)

The attitudinal standpoint that emphasizes success or failure makes a crude assumption that living in the community is in some intrinsic way better than residential care. As we have indicated, this is not necessarily so. Miss Burke shared a house with a friend, who gave her care and support with help from the district nursing service. She had multiple sclerosis and knowing that her condition would worsen she was planning her own admission into residential care. She made applications to the Cheshire Foundation and after visiting a nearby Cheshire Home she described her stay there as 'bloody fantastic'. She explained this reaction by describing how in the Home there was always someone to help her. She fell out of bed while transferring herself to a chair and rang the bell for assistance: she was admonished by the staff that she did not ring more persistently as this was, in the view of the staff, an emergency. She had more the expectations of someone who was used to being left on her own for eight hours in the day and had no objection to waiting. The immediacy of the care provided in the residential setting came as a surprise. The opportunity of going permanently into such care would relieve her anxiety and also take the pressure off her friend. The sociability of residential care also compared favourably with her isolation at home.

Many disabled who are not housebound overcome this isolation by their involvement in the world of the disabled. Mr and Mrs Nichols, both registered blind, feel that they have not suffered from social isolation because they have always been ready to accept help. As other disabled people commented, this sometimes means accepting help when it is not needed. Their overgrown garden, however, was cleared by workers on community service orders. One was so pleased with his work that he came back and has become a friend. They have a lot of contact with children on the estate where they live. The children often talk about them in their presence: 'He's blind. He can't see you. He can't see that ball over there.' When Mr Nichols went to post a letter a little girl took him by the hand. Their social life is limited more by financial stringency than by other factors. Their mobility allowance is sufficient to cover the costs of perhaps two trips by taxi in a week. But they are also able to go to a blind club because transport is arranged by the club.

Mrs Jones, blind, had experienced prejudice in her own family. She had been left alone at social gatherings, as if people did not know how to talk with her. On one occasion she was excluded from the guest list at a wedding: her blindness, accidentally caused, seemed to have the implication of a family curse.

Going to a day centre and mixing with other disabled people offers a refuge where in exchange for accepting a label as 'client', the individual may hope to be 'understood'.

THE DISABLED IDENTITY

In becoming disabled, the individual may have to make a transition from one social network to another, as he takes on a disabled identity. (This is analogous with work: one could well say, for example, that a teacher lives in a world of education, with friends and outside activity often relating to a professional identity – the disabled identity, likewise, may help to create such a social network, where friends are found through the special circumstances of being disabled.)

Taking on a disabled identity is often the hidden task at the centre of able-bodied ideas of rehabilitation – getting people to accept that they are 'disabled' – while the individual retains an idea of himself independent of his disability. Mrs Albury is in her early 60s and for the past 25 years has been suffering from spinal and hip problems. Despite surgery she has been virtually confined to her home for some years. Apart from her husband and other members of the family who did her shopping, cleaning, and other household tasks, Mrs Albury was isolated, no longer seeing former acquaintances. She resisted taking on a disabled identity, even though she seemed to have lost her able-bodied status. She had recently taken the step of applying for a disabled sticker for the car and hoped as a result to be able to visit the shops. But, although lonely and appreciative of an opportunity to talk, Mrs Albury would not consider joining a disabled group or day centre, though her sister who also suffered from a rheumatoid condition did so. Mrs Albury found the prospect of meeting together with other people who were disabled distasteful. She preferred to view her own disability as temporary and placed her hope in a further operation.

Becoming disabled through a progressive disease demonstrates in slow motion the shifting status from able-bodied to disabled. Five years ago Mrs Kane was diagnosed as having multiple sclerosis. At the time she was nearing the end of her time at university and was fortunate in being able to complete her course and graduate. Her final year had been increasingly troubled by symptoms for which her GP could find no explanation other than 'nerves'. As the result of a sudden collapse and temporary paralysis she was admitted to hospital, a diagnosis made and treatment started. She had by this time been accepted by the Civil Service, but as arrangements had not been finalized, the Civil Service declined to offer her a permanent post, offering her instead an unestablished post for a five-year term on the grounds of her being a 'health-risk'.

Although she had some difficulty in walking and using her arms, Mrs Kane was able to get around without aids, and her disability was not immediately apparent. It had come as a surprise to her when a colleague asked if she was getting the mobility allowance, as she had been careful not to let her disability intrude in her work, avoiding asking for help. This area of asking for help or of others offering it she found difficult to handle (on her part, a fear of dependence: on theirs, the fear of intrusion); a wheelchair would simplify the situation – implying a convergence between her own perception of self and others' perception – and then there would be no doubt as to one's needs.

Eighteen months ago, when the MS Society started a local branch, Mrs Kane joined. She has been greatly supported by her parents and husband. Her parents had been active in the

MS Society since her illness was first diagnosed, but Mrs Kane herself resisted any involvement.

> 'To begin with I couldn't think of myself as one of them. I didn't want to know. I wouldn't admit it to myself, but with time you face up to it. Now I almost enjoy belonging to the MS Society, not as a member to be helped, but one to do the helping. You gain a lot in just exchanging experiences, almost a feeling of happiness. . . .'

As her disease has progressed, Mrs Kane has moved from a situation where she wished to be associated only with the able-bodied to an increasing involvement with the disabled. She finds fulfilment in helping others who are either physically more disabled than she is, or who have not yet been able to accept the fact of their illness. In the local branch of the MS Society both Mrs Kane and her husband now take an active part; in addition to her counselling role she assists with administration, fund-raising activities, and meetings.

Taking on a disabled identity is stimulated by relationships with others: it is a reciprocal process. After an accident at work, Mr Sheffield had to give up activities that he enjoyed; dancing and cricket. But he also no longer sees the friends and colleagues with whom he used to share his leisure time. 'If it weren't for caravanning, I'd have nothing. That's my life now.' Interestingly though, the particular friend whom he has made through this activity is also disabled. Through the caravan club, Mr Sheffield and his family have been enabled to share together in the leisure world of the able-bodied – when dances are arranged at sites, Mrs Sheffield is able to participate. Mr Sheffield, at best, can vicariously share in his son's activities: 'I can't play with my son – he never bothers to ask me now. If he wants to play football or cricket I have to rely on others to play with him.' It was a recent remark by his father-in-law that had brought home to Mr Sheffield how others now viewed him, regardless of the image he might wish to cling to himself; one of his father-in-law's friends had been about to hand Mr Sheffield a box to carry when his father-in-law said, 'Don't give it to him, he's a cripple.' 'That's how they must see me. I don't see myself like that but that's how they must see me.'

So when we see the world of the disabled as characterized by a social network, made up partly of professional support and partly of informal care from family and friends, where there is a common identity or identification of the needs of the disabled, where disabled individuals are working out a *modus vivendi* in relation to those upon whom they are dependent for physical care, their success or failure in doing this is dependent on their acceptability, their sensitivity to the use made of them by the able-bodied. To an extent, they are keeping the able-bodied in ignorance of their distress, perhaps through the apparent functioning of the family unit and by making the able-bodied feel good about their ability to co-exist.

Concepts like rehabilitation and integration can be fully understood only with reference to the psychological disturbance the disabled may arouse in the able-bodied. The success of the disabled living in the community has much to do with their ability themselves to contain the anxiety that they engender in those with whom they have quite 'ordinary' relationships in their everyday lives.

DISABILITY AND WORK

The ideas of rehabilitation and adjustment that different people put forward in relation to disability are open to contradictory interpretation. What is being propounded? That disabled people be encouraged and helped to be 'normal' like others? Or to accept that they are different? In our experience disabled people tend to favour the first interpretation, and able-bodied people the second. Certainly, the acceptance of disabled people as 'really normal' does not necessarily extend to seeing them as employable.

Those involved in the education and training of the younger disabled are often working towards quite separate objectives: (a) to help people to live creative and worthwhile lives by encouraging their appreciation of the world around them and (b) make them employable. At a conference on employment and the disabled, the able-bodied speakers were, on the one hand, casting doubt on the continued relevance of what they called the Puritan Work Ethic and, on the other, promoting schemes to develop the competitiveness of young disabled people in the open job market. This ambivalence about objectives demonstrates how the disabled are useful for the exploration of moral and ethical questions that have a wider relevance. The wish of disabled people to be in employment is saying that they want to be valued in the same way as the able-bodied who 'work'. Sheltered workshops and work centres have traditionally met this need of the severely disabled – to the extent that they are now sometimes seen as menial and exploitative. Those making such criticisms no longer value work – any old work – for its own sake.

Such a debate can only be stimulated by rising unemployment. The disabled may even, in such circumstances, be seen as pioneers in a leisure society, where being is more significant than doing. At the same time, the supposed determination of some disabled people to work is seen as an asset, and attributes like punctuality and good attendance are seen as factors to be exploited to their advantage – in contrast to the work-shy able-bodied. The discussion was wide-ranging, a demonstration of the use made, consciously or not, of the disabled for exploration of issues of common human concern.

Advocates of either argument would find supporters among the disabled themselves. Mrs Nichols, with experience of open employment as a telephonist, now thinks that in general it is unrealistic for disabled people to expect to be employed. It would be an unreasonable responsibility to put on the employer. The distribution of attitudes is here such that the employer is seen either to be showing positive discrimination or else to be rejecting. The implied risk is that the employer would be taking no obligations greater than those towards an able-bodied employee. Not only might a disabled person go sick (even when there is no special reason why such a person should go sick) or put in a poor work performance, but the contract of employment becomes confused with a contract of care.

In thinking about the disabled and work, one can think of certain kinds of employment as unsuitable for those with specific difficulties; or that disability is irrelevant to a range of occupations; or that disability can be put to positive use in different kinds of work. A young man confined to a wheelchair wanted to be a motor mechanic. This might be taken as a clear-cut example of the first category (though it is necessary to be careful about this: one of the things we admire in the disabled is the exceptional case, one who has achieved the 'impossible' – and those who do the admiring may be the first to put obstacles in the way). A disabled man working as an accountant or an insurance broker may well have been influenced in choosing that profession because it offers a minimum of physical inconvenience. The content of his work is not greatly affected by his disability – unless, as sometimes happens, he takes on above-average commitments in the voluntary sector.

Some people 'work' at being disabled. Their bookshelves carry books about welfare rights, law, psychology, and sociology. Several of those living in institutions as well as those in their own homes had successfully completed the Open University course *The Handicapped Person in the Community*. One woman had carried out a research project for a voluntary organization: it was a survey of residential care. A man who had lived in institutions and was now in the community had completed a course on community studies. His thesis was: 'Can Institutions be Humanized?' He did not think so, but for purposes of the thesis he came to a more optimistic conclusion – an example of the disabled saying what the able-bodied want to hear.

Miss Lamb, confined to a wheelchair, was active on the boundary of the disabled world, talking at conferences and contributing to seminars of social work students training to work with the disabled. Having herself benefited from counselling at a time of personal crisis she was considering how she might herself develop her expertise and knowledge of the problems facing the disabled in their lives. At one conference where she was making some critical comments about the caring professions, for concentrating on what she could not do rather than on her abilities, she was challenged immediately about her qualifications for saying these things! She could only answer that she had a lifetime as a consumer of the services available to the disabled. Her qualification was, in fact, that she was disabled, and this gave authority to her opinions. But it was also a limiting qualification, as she well realized, and on hearing about other disabled people who had not completed counselling courses she was further uncertain whether they had been discriminated against or had 'failed'. She hoped instead to go for social work training – with a placement in residential care! – as an acceptable way of developing her skills and overcoming the stigma of simply being a consumer.

The counselling of disabled people is a kind of work where being oneself disabled is not necessarily the problem – it could instead be a positive factor. At another conference in counselling we heard the argument that having a similar disability might even be an *essential* qualification for counselling the recently disabled. Here was an indication of the antipathy felt by some disabled people at having their 'problems' projected on to them by the able-bodied.

Disabled applicants for jobs are subject to the reversed binocular vision that in order to show themselves to be really normal they have to show themselves to be special. Mr Nixon was a disabled resident in a local authority home. He applied for the job of clerical officer there. He had already been working in a voluntary way with the previous clerical officer. In going for employment with the local authority – which had an express policy of non-discrimination on the grounds of race, sex, or disability – he was exploring how far his physical limitations could be contained so that he could take up an active, able-bodied status in society. The issues that his application raised had to do with determining his identity as an individual in relation to his environment. Within the residential unit he was testing the artificiality of a clear-cut distinction between staff (able-bodied-normal), and residents (disabled-clients). Even in a culture that was sympathetic to the idea of the disabled retaining personal autonomy, this was a challenge to an organization deriving its structure from just that distinction. Its primary task assumed a group of carers and others dependent on that care. In the dynamic of the institution's activity this application set a problem: as a worker he might have access to confidential information about the residents, both in the administrative work of a clerical officer and also as a member of the staff group. While his application was still in process, there was ambiguity about his attendance at the staff group.

Mr Nixon was seen by the interviewing panel and was accepted for the post, on the understanding that he could do the work with voluntary help. As an employee of the local authority he then had to have a medical examination. The Medical Officer felt unable to pass him as fit for the post – he did not see how a man without the use of his hands could be a clerical officer. This was obviously a question about which there could be two views. Depending on one's view, the Medical Officer was either holding a realistic position, or was a reactionary obstacle to the employment of Mr Nixon. After his application was blocked, the ambivalence about Mr Nixon was no longer apparent in the residential unit; feelings polarized in his support.

But the question of whether an individual is suited to carry out a certain kind of work is never so simple as determining whether he or she has the necessary skills. Those who are employed and become disabled and then want to carry on working are experiencing in their own lives the contrast between open employment as able-bodied and the often precarious positive discrimination as disabled.

Mr Potter, in his early 50s, holds a senior administrative post in the education service. Paraplegic as a result of polio contracted while he was serving with the armed forces during World War II, Mr Potter is for the most part confined to a wheelchair. He receives 100 per cent disability pension and has in addition always been in employment since he left the forces. Currently he faces premature retirement as a result of his disability, and plans to devote even more of his time to furthering the interests of the disabled. In his home town (and, indeed, over a wider area) he is regarded as an authority on disability, sitting on committees, giving talks to community groups, involving himself in attempting to alter legislation, and generally trying to get a better deal for the disabled. He believes there is 'a wall of prejudice against the disabled; they're the only group not protected by law against discrimination'. He thinks the prejudice is based on fear, and can recall his own reactions before the onset of his disability: 'As children we used to cross over the street when we saw a cripple . . . when I was in the ARP I remember helping to get people out of a bombed building and being terrified that they might be damaged, not that they might be dead.'

Following his illness, Mr Potter underwent a protracted

rehabilitation with the emphasis on looking as normal as possible, and wherever possible, on taking part in normal activities: 'You have to look right – if you look right you're accepted by society. You try not to look disabled.' On demobilization he returned to his former employer, a local authority, where he met resistance to being re-employed. However, he insisted on his reinstatement rights and was taken on again, ungraded on a temporary basis. He fought for and obtained a permanent post in the clerical grade. He studied and took exams and after some time was successful in getting an administration post; his disability was not held against him this time, which he attributed to the fact that the principal had experience of disability in his own family.

Clearly, Mr Potter's personality has contributed to 'success'. Opposition or discouragement served only to make him more determined to lead a normal life. 'I've always involved myself, always had a go, so the disability doesn't count. I use my personality to defeat the disability. At work I am accepted for what I am.'

Others were not so resilient, or preferred the protective aspects of disabled living. Mr O'Leary had ambitions to be a social worker but had been turned down. He assumed that this was because of his disability which he saw as a qualification for the job. Since he had become disabled in adult life he had the opportunity to compare from his own experience work in the open market and sheltered workshops. Having himself worked in factories his conclusion was that the disabled did not know when they were well-off. His awareness of the discrimination against the disabled was tempered by his perception of the 'realities' of open employment.

What appeared, initially, to be a small accident at work has left Mr Sheffield, once a foreman, with a permanent disability. He receives a 30 per cent disability pension, moves around inside the house with the aid of crutches, and gets from the house to his car only at the risk of falling over. Operations in the early days of his disability appear to have made him worse and he is currently undergoing a series of operations in order to offset the effects of earlier surgical intervention. He was awarded reduced compensation on the grounds that as foreman he was responsible for ensuring the safety of equipment. Mr Sheffield thinks society is indifferent to people in his position. Various efforts have been made to encourage him to take a retraining course which Mr Sheffield resists. He is not interested in the kinds of jobs for which retraining has been suggested, and he is fearful too of losing his invalidity benefit. If after retraining he found himself unemployed he would be financially worse off than at present. It is difficult for Mr Sheffield to accept the far-reaching effects of his disability – so long as he can hold on to some kind of hope of returning to his former job, or of using his Heavy Goods Vehicle Licence again, he can hold on to his identity as not disabled, or only temporarily so. He resists aids in the home lest he should become too dependent on them. He is in some ways at present negotiating with two identities, slowly assuming the new, unwelcome disabled identity as its realities increasingly impinge on him. Thus he has no wish to register as disabled, but in the home he and his wife have changed roles, Mr Sheffield managing the housework and his wife taking on full-time employment.

Mr Mead is 40. Six years ago MS was diagnosed. By this time he could walk only with the greatest difficulty. Throughout several years of increasing disability, his symptoms had been dismissed as 'nerves', and he had even been thought to be malingering by the Job Centre. This may be a common mis-diagnosis – an able-bodied preference for the label of malingerer rather than of disabled. He was in fact desperately anxious to retain his links with the world of work, but when we saw him he had been unemployed for six months. Prior to this he had worked as manager of a local branch of a national firm. The firm closed down the branch, giving Mr Mead and the rest of the staff no notice of their intention; 'and they didn't pay me a penny more compensation than they had to'. At the time, his disability was so severe that he could get to work only with the aid of a taxi. He was initially refused the mobility allowance, but finally was granted it after the Disablement Resettlement Officer (DRO), the consultant, and his MP had all been involved. Mr Mead felt he was a burden to his family, he was unable to share his children's activities and his wife, he felt, would be better off without him. He had joined the local MS Society and valued his contacts with other members.

A Life Together

Surprisingly, for by this time his disease had progressed to such an extent that his eyesight, memory, arms, legs, and bladder were all affected, Mr Mead managed to find another job. His employers were impressed by his enthusiasm and work-mates volunteered to give him lifts to and from work. Sadly, after only two weeks, his employment was terminated.

The role of the DRO (within the Employment Services Division of the Manpower Services Commission) is important to our understanding of attitudes because of its specialized position on the boundary of the disabled and able-bodied worlds. In the course of our study we were able to see two DROs and some of their clients. We also had several meetings with a Hospital Resettlement Officer. Our discussions with them helped us to examine ideas about the negotiating process by which disabled people succeed or fail in achieving an employable status equivalent to that of the able-bodied.

The DRO is himself in a role that puts him out of the mainstream of the work of his department. We were told that contact between DROs could be infrequent: they are responsible to line managers with other responsibilities and priorities. One DRO felt a lack of recognition of what he was trying to do: 'People in our department don't want to know – there is not much awareness or understanding or even desire to know what goes on, what our problems are.'

The role seemed to encapsulate an ambivalence about the right of disabled people to equal opportunity in the world of work. It has been argued, for example, that the employment quota system is an example of legislation that is detrimental to the interests of disabled people, but is retained, and even fought for, because it has become symbolic of deeply felt values – e.g. that the majority of disabled people are capable of and should have employment on their own merits, provided that prejudice and discrimination are overcome (Bolderson 1980).

One DRO saw as his problem the borderline cases where he was trying to implement a judgement whether clients were employable or not – those who had serious handicaps, but for whom he still had to try and find work. (It was relevant that the 'handicaps' he listed were all of a kind that might show as behavioural problems in the workplace, rather than a physical inability to carry out a task: epileptics, neurotics, those with anxiety states.) His 'selling point' was that some people who were disabled and wanting work would put in that much more effort than an able-bodied person. Effort, though, is not the same as output, and this is one distinction between sheltered workshops and open employment. The DRO had seen a woman with a progressive disease in a workshop laboriously struggling with a routine task. He thought it was extraordinary that she could keep going. It was as if the DRO liked a good tryer.

The DRO might be critical of the financial benefit that disabled people got because the criteria for benefit were different from his own assessment of clients. 'Mobility allowance – some of the most deserving don't get it.' A client had great difficulty in walking, but was not so disabled that he qualified for the allowance. In what sense was he deserving? The DRO explained that the client wanted to work and he had a family to support. He was, however, unable to use public transport and the Department were paying for a taxi, for which he had to pay a contribution as if he were receiving the mobility allowance. The DRO was concerned that if his client lost this job, he would never get another one.

Getting employment for someone who was physically disabled was thus linked in the DRO's mind with motivation. Employment seemed almost to be a reward for the tryers. Those clients who were thought to have psychological problems were not so obviously deserving cases. It was difficult for the DRO to refer such cases to employers without losing credibility.

In talking about their clients the DROs described a workload that was at the same time worth while and yet hopeless. Because many of their clients had mental handicaps and psychological problems, the task of representing their needs was at the least uncomfortable. In the world of work such people might be thought work-shy and unsuitable. The DROs did not think it was possible (or right) to put pressure on employers. In their view the poor administration of the quota system was evidence of this: better that some employers were very helpful – perhaps because they themselves had family experience of disability – and one was grateful to them.

The disabled seeking work are having to tread the middle

ground: on the one hand they are being judged on their motivation, on the other they are not expected to show evidence of material success. A DRO visited a client at home: 'It's better than my own'. And the DRO saw as part of the job a policing of the welfare system so that clients did not take unfair advantage of the provision they were enjoying.

In summary, the question of work stimulates ambivalence both among disabled people and others about their dependent status in society. Some are reluctant to pursue work if this might undermine their rights to financial support – for example, where they have compensation claims to be determined. And more than once we heard the opinion that at a time of high unemployment the disabled do not have the same right to work as the able-bodied.

FINANCIAL PROVISION

The first thing anyone is told about the welfare rights aspect of disabled living is that it is very complex. Those experiencing its complexity find it mystifying and inconsistent. This is not the place to attempt our own exegesis. However, we may wonder how this complexity – the illogicalities of historical precedent tidied up by the bureaucratic mind – relates to different attitudes towards disability; and also what effect this complexity has on the ways disabled people relate to their environment.

Several factors contribute to the complexity. The attempt to be fair, realistically to compensate for the costs of disability, is hedged about with caveats. It is equality of a kind that the disabled have to tighten their belts 'like everyone else' at a time of economic recession. It is fair in a way that the victim of an industrial accident should receive compensation, although in effect this discriminates against those who are disabled in circumstances outside the jurisdiction of the courts or the policies of insurance companies. Advice services and literature on financial benefits proliferate, and give employment and opportunities for the development of special expertise to the able-bodied and disabled alike. The annual *Disability Rights Handbook* of the Disability Alliance is a best-seller – 15–20,000 copies a year. The Disablement Income Group (DIG) has leaflets on: attendance allowance, mobility allowance, sickness and invalidity benefit, non-contributory invalidity pensions, non-contributory invalidity pensions for married women, invalid care allowance, exceptional circumstances additions, supplementary benefit appeal tribunals, and, of course, the Chronically Sick and Disabled Persons Act 1970.

It has been argued by Topliss and others that this Act had a humanitarian base but has run foul of economic arguments (Topliss 1979). It was drafted at a time of economic optimism, on the assumption that an advanced industrial Western nation could and should afford to provide for the needs of its disabled population. But social provision for the poor and disadvantaged has historically always been linked to the economic interest, and humane legislation on behalf of the deserving poor has implicitly the economic advantage of encouraging them to be self-sufficient and so less passively dependent on the common wealth of the nation.

So we may ask how the complexity of getting financial benefit matches up to the confusing ambiguities of trying to meet people's dependency needs and at the same time help them to be independent. It is a problem for any kind of 'welfare', and not only to do with the disabled. (For example, how do you help poor people without waiting for them to be destitute and thus, in effect, asking them to prove that they cannot cope before offering the means by which they might cope?) We may wonder how far in getting one's rights as a disabled person one may feel schizoid – having to prove oneself in a dependent role – not only physically but emotionally and socially – in order to achieve a measure of financial independence.

The complexity of getting benefit has to do with the different standards being implied. Economist commentators have identified three different principles: insurance, relief, and compensation (Simkins and Tichner 1978). Invalidity benefit is an example of insurance, as are old age pensions or widows' benefit. Where the insurance is inadequate, it has to be supplemented by relief – supplementary benefit, with note taken of exceptional circumstances and needs. The compensatory principle is different, and it is a principle that has been more widely applied in recent years. Compensation for industrial injury has obvious justification, though it does not have the social-class related benefit – as for those injured while serving in

97

the armed forces who are compensated both according to the degree of disability and also in relation to rank. But there is also compensation in response to special need, including the attendance allowance, invalid care allowance, and of course mobility allowance.

The complexity of financial benefit thus derives from the apparent difficulty in determining a single principle – say, need. That, in itself, would be difficult enough to sort out. But other principles – to do with the cause and context of disability or monitoring the position of a disadvantaged group dependent on society – introduce constraints and exceptions, discrimination, and tests of eligibility that to the consumer seem to have little to do with need.

One effect of legislation and the process of getting benefit is to institutionalize difference. Miss White has multiple sclerosis; after a period in residential care, she is now living independently in a council flat. After two years of receiving mobility allowance, she has been further assessed. Her feelings about this were mixed. She did not want to lose the mobility allowance, but she thought that she was at the moment walking better than for five years. The outcome of the assessment was thus both satisfactory and depressing: she was to receive the allowance for the full statutory term, i.e. until she was seventy-five. She was disabled for life: the financial benefit was confirmation of the medical diagnosis.

The therapeutic ambition of able-bodied towards the disabled – encouraging their integration and adjustment and rehabilitation and so on – may lead to attempts to put constraints on benefit in order not to confirm people in a disabled dependent role. Thus it is not inconsistent according to this argument for a surgeon working with spinal cord injured patients to act as a consultant also for insurance companies seeking to limit the extent of claims. In both cases he is working to an idea of the disabled as living as normally as possible, and not sheltering unnecessarily behind their disabled status.

Often the experience of getting the financial benefit is thought of as an achievement in itself. In applying for mobility allowance, Mrs Thompson was seen first by a doctor who thought she was eligible, and then by a medical panel, who refused her application. She appealed against this decision, and after eighteen months of trying she received the benefit.

Financial provision – or the lack of it – is thus inextricably a part of the 'disabled identity', helping to determine the status of the individual as a disabled person. Mr Sheffield had a friend who was an amputee. To his own mind he was less obviously disabled, and as his friend had been refused, he did not at first think of applying for the mobility allowance for himself. The wish to assert independence may even lead to an inhibition in claiming benefit, like the woman caring for a dependent relative who refuses to see himself as an invalid, and who therefore does not claim the invalid care allowance.

There has to be some system of qualifying for benefit, and perhaps there always has to be a seeming element of grudging charity. But it is important to recognize the symbolic quality of any kind of assessment, however necessary, and to question vigorously how necessary really are some of the hoops that people are put through before they can have the help that it is generally agreed they should have as a right. Bureaucratic caution can also be an effective if unconscious carrier of punitive social values, discriminating against those who ambivalently in our society are the objects of care and suspicion.

THE CARE RELATIONSHIP – TWO EXAMPLES

When we speak of improving attitudes we may most often be thinking of winning over those who reject the disabled, who overtly express hostility, or who show indifference to their situation. We would now like to examine the attitudes that emerge in interactions between those who seek to help and be involved and the disabled who are the recipients of the help. In any interaction between physically handicapped and able-bodied, a whole complex gamut of emotions and attitudes intervenes. The way in which a helper thinks he views disability and the way in which those he seeks to help view the disability may be quite different from the non-verbal content of the transaction.

The disabled person too may be projecting into a transaction his own negative feelings about a spoilt identity and the dependent position in which he finds himself. Perhaps the greatest difficulty lies in holding on to projections (on either side) and owning them. For those who are well disposed towards the disabled a crucial dilemma seems to arise in accepting the disabled as a whole person. By that we mean accepting both the dependent parts of that person, as well as the independent parts – as distinct from a spurious picture of wholeness that denies the dependency.

In the world of the disabled, there are examples of social organization, clubs, outings, holidays, which demonstrate both a desire to integrate disabled people by allowing them opportunities for social integration and to discriminate positively to compensate for their disability.

(a) Physically Handicapped and Able Bodied – a model of integration

Living in the community can mean very little more than living at home as opposed to living in an institution. Segregation in terms of leisure, for example, is the norm, with special clubs provided by the able-bodied for the disabled. Instead of sharing the leisure activities of the rest of society the disabled tend to be hived off to spend their time together. Many welcome this. In one club with an elderly clientele, many of whom lived alone and were entirely dependent on home helps and neighbours, the once-weekly club meeting and the day centre provided their only outings. Sales of groceries and small items at the club meant they were a little less dependent on neighbours. At the day centre they were able to have a meal – an appreciable benefit when the exertion required to cook was considerable. One woman was too badly crippled by arthritis even to make a cup of tea and used a thermos in between visits from neighbours and home help. Another who lived alone got herself to bed by means of a hoist. Club outings and holidays provided much needed breaks.

We did not come across clubs formed by the disabled and run entirely by them. Instead we saw how the able-bodied start the ball rolling, find premises, arrange transport, canvass for membership, and lay on activities.

PHAB clubs were initiated when a disabled youngster found

herself excluded from the activities of a conventional youth club. The club leader wished to avoid segregation and based clubs on the notion of physically handicapped and able-bodied coming together – hence the name – initially in equal numbers, to pursue common interests. Now a national voluntary organization, PHAB aims to build bridges between able-bodied and physically handicapped. It is in a sense providing a kind of rarefied atmosphere in which 'really normal' aspects of the physically handicapped may be encouraged.

'Whether you are able-bodied or physically handicapped you will meet on equal terms to develop and share your common interests and you will be actively engaged in destroying the barriers erected by fear, insecurity and prejudice that prevent integration.'   (PHAB 1977)

'Integration for the disabled' (says another account) 'means a thousand things. It means the absence of segregation, it means being able to be treated like everybody else. It means the right to work, to go to cinemas, to enjoy outdoor sport, to have a family life and a social life and a love life, to contribute materially to the community, to have the usual choices of association, movement and activity, to go on holiday to the usual places, to be educated up to university level with one's unhandicapped peers, to travel without fuss on public transport. Whatever their different circumstances all disabled people yearn for a society which palpably recognizes its common humanity with the handicapped.'
(Snowdon 1976)

It would seem then that in the micro-climate of a PHAB club the world might see how life could be lived, with the differences between physically handicapped and able-bodied no longer forming a barrier to each seeing the other as 'real'. Is a PHAB club the model for integration? Is it a place where the 'right' attitudes are being displayed, or is it a variation on the traditional club where the able-bodied provide special services for the disabled? Is the wider community in which the club is situated influenced by the club's activities? Does the club perhaps simply serve to take the heat off the community – is it a refined and improved form of segregation? Different local communities, it seems, react in different ways to their disabled members. Some clubs were well supported while others were neglected to such an extent that they seriously questioned whether they could continue. We visited two clubs which had totally different experiences of community support.

Both of these were junior clubs. Club A had experienced problems from the outset; the first difficulty had been finding premises for the club. A letter to the Social Services Department in this connection had been ignored, as had a letter to a special school for the disabled. A local Youth Officer had suggested the school hall where the group now met. Initially children at this school had shown great enthusiasm for the project, but since the club could take only a limited number of the able-bodied, the majority of those wishing to be involved could not be accommodated. Some eighteen months later the number of able-bodied members was fewer than the number of physically handicapped, some of the able-bodied being siblings of the disabled. The club leaders organized transport for both the disabled and the able-bodied ('so that there is no discrimination'), and this was an activity which involved them in very considerable effort. An ambulance had to be borrowed from a neighbouring borough and returned there after all the children had been returned to their homes. One of the leaders left his employment early on club day and spent the greater part of the evening, usually until after midnight, in transport arrangements. Fund-raising activities also presented difficulties and had even, on occasion, to be cancelled due to lack of support. The parents of the disabled youngsters were said to be indifferent to the club's activities, not wishing to be involved in fund-raising or even in seeing the premises. The leaders did not wish to take undue advantage of the few parents who were helpful.

By contrast, Club B, which also met in a school hall, received borough support. Two ambulances were provided so the leaders were relieved of the responsibility of getting children to the club. Ambulance personnel joined in club activities for part of the time. Here, too, parents showed indifference but from the leader's viewpoint this was offset by support from the club's committee. But in neither club was there a great deal of evidence of meaningful interaction between able-bodied and disabled children, though in Club B there was a greater degree of sharing. Even here, a hockey-type game resulted in most of the physically handicapped being stranded, while the active children played the game around them, passing the ball to a handicapped child when reminded to do so by the adults. Differences in motor ability between the two groups meant that in reality there were limitations to the pursuits that could be shared.

Many of us find it difficult to bear the helplessness which accompanies disability. There are several mechanisms by which we escape facing this, perhaps the most usual being in a group setting where hectic programmes of activities are laid on. A journalist's account of a PHAB club illustrates the kind of thing we have in mind:

> 'Myra had just returned from a week's PHAB course when I met her and I was fascinated by the itinerary – especially as the youngsters on the course were all severely handicapped.
>
> They had been to the theatre, visited the Navy, gone on a scavenger hunt and been riding. . . . The highlight of the week was a motor-bike scramble and a bonfire. The handicapped were strapped to the rear seat of the motor-bike and off they roared.'

The description of the club continues:

> 'All around me were scenes that wouldn't look out of place at an ordinary party. A spastic boy was doing his best to chat up a pretty girl. . . . As the sky darkened . . . the music got louder . . . everyone sang and danced – with their hands, if they couldn't dance with their feet. It was an evening out with people, fit or otherwise, enjoying themselves together.'
>
> (*Woman's Realm* 1978)

Exciting and inspiring accounts of the activities of clubs or day centres, minimizing the effects of disability or implying that with the right attitude and sufficient goodwill severe physical handicap could be overcome, are attractive. But, as we found, clubs for the disabled are not simply places of goodwill, full of keen and active members enjoying each other's company. (In one very poorly attended adult club, the only able-bodied member was the leader.) The helper may well be

103

moved by compassion, may wish to help those less fortunate than himself ('having been one of the lucky ones, I have always tried to find ways to put something back into life – how lucky we who are whole are'), and at the same time demand, usually quite unconsciously, something in return from those he is helping. The very act of helping may confer on an individual a status in the community, may make him feel worth while. In this case the act of helping is a reward in itself. But it means that for his own self-esteem the helper needs the one he is helping, perhaps as much as the latter needs him.[1]

(b) Positive discrimination – a holiday for the disabled

The disabled of one London Borough are eligible to go on an annual holiday organized by the Social Services Department – in this case, in association with a voluntary body. This is an example of a compensatory service where evidence of disadvantage allows compensatory advantage. Whatever the statutory responsibility of the local authority, the holiday has the appearance of being different from other services, domiciliary help, or day centre provision. It is more than a privilege, but somehow less than a right.

How does this happen? Being disabled, the individual is at a disadvantage. Attempts to compensate for that disadvantage in different ways – whether it is by putting stickers on cars to give privilege on the roads, a quota system for employment, or otherwise alleviating reversible distress associated with disability – have the effect of confirming the status of disability at the same time as doing something about its effects.

We were told a personal anecdote that illustrates the ambivalent balance of rights and privilege. A disabled music lover wanted to go to a concert. Being disabled he was eligible for a reduction on the price of his ticket, but it was only possible for him to take up this privilege if he was accompanied by an escort. He preferred to go on his own. Although he was in a

[1] Arabic law appears to recognize this more overtly than we do. Thus visitors to Saudi Arabia are warned against helping the victim of, say, a road accident. The helper – regardless of whether he was to blame for the accident or merely a by-stander – by the very act of helping assumes a continuing responsibility for the victim.

wheelchair he was able to do this; but he had to pay the full price – the price of being normal.

In similar ways – and a holiday for the disabled may be one – the disabled who take advantage of opportunities made available to them are possibly paying a hidden cost to do with their accepting a dependent culture. Positive discrimination of this kind further illustrates the ambivalences in the care relationship and the contradictions of being both really normal and special. The collaboration between voluntary and statutory services in administering the holiday for the disabled was itself an indication that the holiday was seen as a local authority responsibility but also a bit special.

Approximately two hundred disabled people went to a coastal holiday camp. They were registered disabled, some with other family members as escorts. There were some elderly from local authority residential care. A group of mentally handicapped came from their residential unit. The majority, though, came from their own homes. Some knew each other from their attendance at day centres or from other contacts in the world of the disabled. Others only met each year on holiday. In effect, the holiday was a coming together of disabled 'living in the community' in the temporary 'institution' of the holiday camp. The helpers were described as volunteers but in different ways they were associated directly with the disabled. Several were social workers, including an assistant director of social services. The clients from Part 3 accommodation were accompanied by their 'matrons'. The mentally handicapped were looked after by their own staff. There were familiar faces from day centres. Even the odd ones out among the helpers had their own idiosyncratic links with the world of the disabled. For example, the son of the chairperson of the voluntary body organizing the holiday and, as it happened, a research worker studying the distribution of attitudes around the disabled. . . .

This last volunteer was given a piece of concrete advice before setting out on the holiday: 'Don't let them take advantage of you!' The politics of the care relationship were thus succinctly expressed. The holiday itself was run with great enthusiasm and expertise. The staff of the holiday camp joined with the local authority and the voluntary group in

A Life Together

providing for the physical needs of the people on holiday and in providing entertainment and a holiday atmosphere. The helper could not fail to feel useful. High sills on the chalets, steep ramps to the main halls, difficult access to the camp shop – all the usual environmental constraints on mobility of the disabled – ensured that his able-bodiedness would always be in demand.

But the physical care – even the intimate care to do with dressing, washing, or going to the toilet – was not the most stressful aspect of the work. He was more aware of the emotional stress of subjugating his own needs, or realizing them through the help he was giving to others. (No doubt different people respond in their own ways. In this case the helper found that he was always hungry; a gut feeling that he also wanted looking after?)

This helper certainly experienced a multi-variant set of relationships. At one moment he felt like a son or grandson showing consideration to an old woman, the next he was swapping jokes with an extrovert housewife or listening to a proposal of marriage from a mentally handicapped woman or wondering how necessary it was to take notice yet again of the repeated complaining of a sad old man. If he had been a professional worker with the disabled, he would perhaps have developed a way of containing the experience and so modifying the extremes. 'You have to treat them the same.' Over a limited period of one week he was able to give physical care as best he could – as he hoped, without discriminating – while retaining a sense of his own splitting of positive and negative feelings towards disabled people.

The fact that he could feel so differently – and the effort of compensating in order to be fair – meant that he could hold attitudes towards the disabled that were quite at variance without having to resolve the contradictions of his position. On the one hand, he could feel for the old woman in her isolation and vulnerability. On the other, he resented what seemed to be an implied criticism of him for being able-bodied by the way the man asked for his help with exaggerated politeness. The subjectivity of the experience did not take away its force, and the experience of working with these two holiday-makers was replicated and further reinforced in his relationships with many others. Going on a shopping expedition, the helper struggled to push a wheelchair through a crowded market. He was aware of his irritation as an escort towards the disabled shopper who insisted on going to every stall, and his simultaneous anger towards the other shoppers who indifferently got in the way.

Talking with holiday-makers often served as an antidote to the somewhat manic feeling of activity and bustle in the events of the day. A woman talking of her family was near to tears: she would have liked to have been with her son and not with strangers. 'But strangers care more than family.'

A man stared out of the coach window at a churchyard:

'How many people do you think there are dead in there?'

'I don't know.'

'All of them!'

This lugubrious joke was the more effective as it was the first unsolicited comment he had made after some hours with the helper. A woman declined meals and lay withdrawn on her bed. A group of disgruntled men swore that they would never go on one of these holidays again – but then they complained every year, so it was said. In contrast, another man said that it was not right to complain, after all the work that people had put in: 'and if you did complain, you might not be accepted next year'.

A holiday camp offers an organized holiday. So there is already a culture consistent with the maintenance of a dependency relationship between the helpers and the clients. For example, the most obvious act like pushing a wheelchair, was helping – but it was also controlling. The helper was enabling the holiday-maker to have a good time, but he was also part of the management of the holiday. For a brief period he was experiencing for himself as a holiday volunteer some of the issues about the care relationship that professional residential care staff have to resolve all the time (as described in Chapter 3).

It follows that the disabled themselves, though on holiday, were still subject to the restrictions of the care relationship, as they experienced it during the other weeks in the year. The helper failed to persuade one holiday-maker to shelter from the wind: she was waiting for Matron. Holiday-makers coming from their own homes also were aware of familiar faces from social services.

In one sense it was obviously their holiday. As an annual event it was eagerly over-subscribed. Like all holidays, the anticipation and the memories were a significant part of the experience. But there was another aspect – secondary perhaps, but important: there was a sense in which clients were there to show their gratitude to the social services. In discussions with the organizers of the holiday, both in the local authority and the voluntary group, we were told about the holiday with pride and enthusiasm. On the holiday itself, the helper was made aware of the need to put on a good show. The anxiety was not so much that the holiday-makers might not enjoy themselves – any dissatisfactions were put down to the idio-syncrasies of clients who had problems – it was that the holiday should be a demonstration that the local authority really cared.

This aspect of the holiday became dominant for a time, on the day of an official visit by the Mayor, the Chairman of the Social Services Committee, the Chairperson of the Association for the Disabled, and the Director of Social Services (himself a helper in previous years). The visit had mixed reactions, both among the helpers and the holiday-makers. The organizers arranged entertainments that would be appropriate for the occasion – for example, a fancy dress parade to be judged by the Mayor. For many people it was an opportunity to shake hands with the Director, well known to them, and exchange a few words. The helpers were instructed to stay on the camp and not – as was usual in the afternoons – to act as escorts for anyone going for a walk or to the shops. Some felt angry – surprising to themselves – at what they felt was the irrelevance of this visit: they made associations in their minds with a seigneurial social system. At the same time, a few holiday-makers deliberately kept away and there were harsh comments about putting on a performance.

If the helper was there to enable the holiday-makers to have a good time, he was also expected to enjoy himself – in fact to have fun on their behalf. There was a tradition – orally transmitted from year to year – of fun and games among the helpers, ducking in the swimming pool, dressing up, making apple-pie beds, and so on. The physical vigour associated with the fun seemed to invite comparison with the limited mobility of disabled people.

The holiday thus had a symbolic meaning: it was psychologically important as a demonstration both of the 'invisible' presence of disabled people living in the community, and as a recognition of all the work that is done on their behalf. It was also a re-affirmation of the nature of the relationship between the disabled and those who represented their interests, with the elements of care and concern, dependency, protectiveness, and of negotiating a balance between enabling and control.

5

The distribution and redistribution of attitudes

One of the difficulties that we envisaged in setting out on this work was the making of generalizations. This was to be a study of attitudes towards or about the physically disabled. We were content to wait to discover what meaning people gave to that term. There are, as we have seen, statutory and administrative definitions, apparently specific; but overlapping with these and using the same terminology are popular definitions, which are not quite the same: for example they exclude invisible or unknown handicaps. By whatever set of criteria, 'the disabled' covers an enormous range of different people with all human characteristics and with all possible malfunctions departing from some supposed norm of the able-bodied – which able-bodied people themselves would spell out differently – ranging from Venus and Adonis to ordinary people, who somehow cope. There are those who, whatever their personal characteristics, may have some minor defect of motor ability, hardly noticeable to the casual observer, through to those with extremes of physical immobility and dependence. But even to think in terms of a continuum from a minor constraint through to total physical dependence is not itself sufficient. In what sense can we seriously lump together those who are blind with those who have motor neuron disease? Or those who are subject to epileptic fits and those who have spinal cord injury? Those who were congenitally deformed and those who have suffered injury in later life? And even within a disability, say cerebral palsy, there are those who have speech and those who do not. Many (estimated between 80–90 per cent) of the disabled – according to statutory criteria – are elderly, and they influence our stereotypes for the old, and may themselves prefer to be thought of as elderly rather than as disabled. Yet a disability that is a taken-for-granted corollary of ageing may be

110

felt as a severe handicap by an active young person. Our feelings about children are also different: the handicapped child is the object of special consideration. For all the diversity, the physically disabled adult is in a minority within a wider context of exceptions to ordinary able-bodied living. So to talk of 'the disabled' is immediately to expose oneself to the absurdity of making generalizations.

Disabled writers and researchers question 'able-bodied' assumptions about problems of body image and so on, when the problems they experience are of others' response to their disability (Oliver 1978). They are making articulate a feeling of disabled people that the problem they face is not that of being disabled themselves but of having to live with able-bodied people, who cannot understand what it is like to be disabled and so unthinkingly 'put them away' in some all-inclusive category of deviance.

The distribution of attitudes shows that the disabled are used as readily available containers of the anxiety that people have about psychological damage. Negotiations between individuals and groups help to outline a disabled identity that is acceptable to the able-bodied. The disabled thus offer a model or rather a variety of models dramatically illustrative of the human condition. (Although, as mentioned in Chapter 1, there seems to have been a recent crop of plays on this theme, it is also the case that disability has been a theme in drama and literature from *Oedipus* through to *Richard III* and to *The Idiot*.) Moreover attitudes are also functional, as Katz has argued (Katz 1960). Their usefulness is expressed in the ways that they justify behaviour – supporting existing practice, inter-preting it to oneself as reasonable, reinforcing one's sense of worth, and explicating it to the outside world.

In this study, we have explored the relationship of the individual to society. Because the individual is disabled, the relationship tests our assumptions about criteria for accept-ance in society. But the criteria remain obscure. So the disabled are not the clearly differentiated group (or groups, allowing for different disabilities) that we imagine. They are to be found as sub-sets among the disadvantaged; among the unemployed, or the physically ill, or the socially isolated. They exist also in their own right(s) as 'disabled' because of the provisions of the legislation applicable to the 'disabled', within which they are differentiated according to mixed criteria of need and eligibility. Both the statutory lumping together and the clumsy mix of criteria are, of course, a reflection of societal attitudes.

THE POLITICS OF IDENTITY

In examining 'attitudes' and 'attitude change' – whatever specific meanings we may assign to these terms – we must ultimately be focusing on relationships in which the presence or absence of disability – again, however that may be defined – is perceived by one or both parties as being an element in the relationship. This may be a relationship between 'able-bodied' and 'disabled'; or one disabled person and another, where disability is an overt or covert element; or two or more 'able-bodied' people who meet in the context of relatedness to an absent 'disabled' individual or group.

Use of inverted commas indicates that the meaning of these terms – 'attitude', 'disabled', 'able-bodied' etc. – is not to be taken for granted; it is problematic. Another way of putting this is to say that, whilst a notion of 'disability' is a determining or at least significant factor in each one of these relationships, the meanings assigned to that term are likely to be more implicit than explicit – hence to be inferred from behaviour rather than merely derived from statements of belief or intention – and also may or may not be reciprocally congruent among the parties involved.

Any relationship may be conceptualized as a transaction across boundaries. Minimally it is a transaction across the personal (psychological) boundaries of the parties to the transaction. Beyond that there are institutionalized role boundaries – e.g. between patient and nurse, client and social worker. Other roles are less institutionalized and more implicit. They derive from wider societal definitions of 'disabled' and 'able-bodied' which the parties represent or – to be more accurate – believe themselves to be representing. 'Benefactor', 'crusader', 'grateful recipient', and 'victim' might be examples. However, such bald terms may over-simplify what are often more complex and subtle role formulations.

The Distribution and Redistribution of Attitudes

At the level of the psychology of interpersonal relations, any transaction between two individuals involves negotiating – and, in any sustained relationship, constantly re-negotiating – two boundaries: between 'me' and 'not-me', and between 'us' and 'not-us'. Some agreement about the us/not-us boundary is a necessary condition for the relationship. The agreement may be explicit or tacit. (To take an extreme example, in the mugger–victim relationship, there is an assumption that the environment offers no threat to the one and no help to the other.) Within that boundary a psychological negotiation occurs between the two parties, each striving to ensure that his picture of the other's picture of him fits with his own picture of himself. This can be thought of as the politics of identity. The goodness of fit that produces a feeling of stability involves conscious and unconscious factors. This complicates the politics of inter-personal relations, since our unconscious wishes may be at loggerheads with what we say and believe. Overtly, for example, we may seek an egalitarian relationship and may have repressed a discreditable wish that the other should look up to us and be dependent on us; but that latter wish, now unconscious, still demands fulfilment; and so we shall not feel totally comfortable unless the other either unconsciously needs the reciprocal relationship or is able to simulate the need. The transaction is characterized by a process of splitting and projection.

In reality we can never relate to the other as someone separate, 'out there': we relate only to the picture of the other that we have in our mind. What the other actually does and says is filtered not only through our perceptual apparatus of ears and eyes but also through our mental classificatory apparatus. Our picture of the other is to a lesser or greater extent blurred and modified by pictures of previous others, compared with whom we perceive this other as similar or dissimilar by criteria that are only partly accessible to us: and we also superimpose on the relationship images of previous relationships that we identify as dynamically similar to this one. Hence our discreditable wish is not only split off from our consciousness but also projected onto the other.

So there is the more general hypothesis that the drawing of the two sets of boundaries – me/not-me and us/not-us – always involves splitting and projection. The ideal of the mature relationship in which fantasy has been ousted by reality may be well worth struggling towards, but it remains nonetheless an unattainable ideal. There is, however, a lot of evidence to support the proposition that there is an inverse relation between the degree of splitting occurring at these two boundaries. The most familiar example is the common enemy: if we agree to project negative feelings into a specified not-us, we experience the other as less theatening to our own identity, the me/not-me boundary is less problematic, and hence there is greater scope for a collaborative relationship to develop between us. Our experience is of a transaction that is positive, constructive, and reality-based; but this is achieved through splitting off and projecting the negative and investing the not-us with our fantasy. Not-us does not have to be an enemy; a similar effect can be attained if we can derive a shared identity from a not-us whom we agree to be different from us – though usually a negative value is assigned to the difference. If on the other hand the us/not-us boundary remains problematic – if there is difficulty in agreeing on its position and its meaning – then the politics of identity in the me/not-me relationship are intensified. I have a greater need to project split-off aspects of me onto the other as not-me. It may then be possible to reach a more genuinely reality-based sense of us – an us that does not rely upon using a not-us as a receptacle for negative feeling, but it will be a more turbulent conflictual relationship. Thus whilst mugger and victim may 'agree' that the environment is not going to intervene in that transaction, they attach polarized meanings to the non-intervening environment: for the one it is benign, for the other malign.

When two 'able-bodied' meet, the 'disabled' are an absent not-us that clearly define the us/not-us boundary (and correspondingly the 'able-bodied' are the absent not-us in the meeting of the 'disabled'). The relationship at least starts from the shared assumption that difference lies outside the boundary and sameness within. To some degree the parties can believe that they are operating with a shared definition of handicap not only as a physical attribute but also as a psycho-social condition: they are dependent (on us); they need (our) care and support. By inference, we are robust, autonomous, secure. Commonly then there is a shared projection onto the absent handicapped of weakness and inadequacy. In fact, of course, the two parties will differ in their fantasies, projections, and the meanings they assign to the boundary, and these differences may be quite quickly exposed; but equally, if both parties have a strong psychological investment in the us/not-us boundary, such differences can remain permanently unvoiced and unexamined: we all know what we mean by 'the disabled', don't we?

However, in the relationship where one party is 'able-bodied' and the other 'disabled' the starting-point is difference; the us/not-us boundary that has to contain the differences is much more elusive. For the relationship to be sustained the reciprocal projections have to be mutually acceptable. Both the structure of the situation and the overtness of the difference encourage each party to define his own identity by quite powerful projection of not-me onto the other; the unacceptable – or wished for – aspects of me that I now perceive in the other tend to polarize us; the polarization generates guilt and anxiety; and secondary defences tend to get mobilized to repress and deny the splitting. Suppression of some feelings and repression of others can thus produce a relationship that is tolerable; but it is unlikely to be comfortable.

IDENTITY AND DAMAGE

The sense of being crippled inside is, we suggest, an aspect of everyday existence, and is not limited to those who demonstrate physical disability.

Sometimes people say that the disabled make them feel guilty. The disturbance caused by confrontation with damage in others can take contradictory forms: sympathy for those less fortunate than oneself; defensiveness as if the disability is contagious and one might become affected in some way by association; antipathy towards those whose disability is seen as an attack on one's able-bodiedness – if the disabled is normal, then the able-bodied feels like a freak. But these reactions have something in common – a realization that the disabled stir up feelings in others. One can seek to moderate these effects by doing something positive – people in wheelchairs know what it is like to be grabbed from behind in the street by well-meaning strangers. An honest recall of one's emotions may reveal to anyone used to being with disabled that at times one's feelings are embarassingly sanctimonious – to feel good towards someone is evidence to oneself of the strength of one's own identity; one is managing the boundary around one's self in a way that allows for the other to be different. (There is, though, another way of interpreting this feeling, in that the disabled other becomes like an extension of one's self, and by looking after the other, one is looking after oneself.)

However, despite the range of issues to do with individual circumstances, dynamics of relationships around people who are disadvantaged through physical dependence have a certain coherence. The core of this argument can be put simply. We impose *our* reality on people as a condition of helping them.

To be disabled means that where there is a recognition of difference based on the disablement of one party in the relationship, there is a demand for positive discrimination to do something about that difference. It happens within the family dynamic as much as it may in political debates to do with social policy. We allow disabled people a limited ability that then requires our assistance in order to fulfil the potential of that ability in meeting their needs as members of our society. In this sense the disabled represent an opportunity to do good. There is what we might call the Good Samaritan syndrome. When we see people who are, on the evidence, disadvantaged in relation to ourselves we may or may not respond from our advantaged position. Very often, of course, we do not react, we accept it as a normal state of affairs.

It is possible psychologically to tolerate inequalities in society, to accept the quality of life for those who are disadvantaged as being at a different level from those who are able to take an active economic role in society. The disadvantaged are not expected to have the same freedom of choice in negotiating their own status, both economic and social, and in this sense having control or influence over the determination of their self-image. It is accepted that disability has social disadvantages as if this were irretrievable. But we become concerned about the disadvantaged when we feel that they are at risk. Take the example of the drunk asleep on a park bench. He may arouse all kinds of feelings in us ranging from disgust to sympathy. We may think of intervening, and yet worry about getting involved. Perhaps he is better off where he is? But if we introduce the element of risk, that the man looks ill and may require medical treatment – is, say, at risk of exposure or perhaps is suffering from other (self-inflicted?) effects of alcoholism – then we might well be happier about intervening, if it means that the drunk will be cared for in hospital. We find the drunk unsettling, disturbing, and to an extent we would like him taken out of our sight. But the important motivation leading to action is the thought that he might be at risk. It is one thing to pass by a drunk in the street and experience a confusing mix of emotions. It is quite another to hear the next day that he is dead.

Our hypothesis – and this is what we mean by the Good Samaritan syndrome – is that faced with evidence of disability and dependency in another, we have a tendency to take on a responsibility for the other. We can tolerate this without acting on it as long as we also hold on to a belief that the other is responsible for himself. If the other comes to harm, however, our feelings of responsibility then become overwhelming. It is our fault now that the drunk is lying on the bench.

We are talking here about a balance of responsibility. Where that balance becomes disrupted, we feel an unbearable guilt. It is guilt as much as altruism that is the motivation that gives us authority to intervene in the life of others. We are not responsible in a full sense for others if they are simply worse off than ourselves. However, if we do nothing and they then suffer in a dramatic and obvious sense, then our feeling of guilt makes us responsible. We realize that we have authority to intervene, like the Good Samaritan.

We help someone across the road not simply because he wants to get across the road but because we fear that he would get knocked down in the attempt on his own. We provide residential care for the disabled because we fear the effects of social isolation on them if they were exposed to ordinary living conditions – we would always be passing by on the other side. We set up sheltered work situations to protect the disabled from the insecurities and stresses of ordinary work. We even

117

discourage the disabled from marriage and sexual relationships because of the dangers inherent in the breakdown of that relationship. We cannot bear to fail them and so we do not even let them try.

So there is after all something coherent about the apparently disparate,and confused concept of disability. It has to do with the boundary around self. In general terms, each of us allows others the freedom to make their own decisions, to succeed or fail. The politics of identity become important when we seek to impose our own values, aims, and objectives on others. In our relationships with the disabled such politics are immediately evident. They must not take risks for themselves as we will feel responsibility if they fail. We work out this in a number of ways – for example, by denying their individuality or by seeing them as mentally defective. We give them the kind of care that diminishes their sense of personal autonomy. They learn to live in environments where we can exercise this responsibility on their behalf.

It is relevant here to link these ideas with Melanie Klein's description of the reparative defence mechanisms that the individual employs to restore a good internal object and reduce one's sense of guilt. 'Side by side with the destructive impulses in the unconscious mind both of the child and the adult, there exists a profound urge to make sacrifices, in order to help and put right loved people who in phantasy have been harmed or destroyed' (Klein and Riviere 1937). However, she also made the distinction with manic reparation, where the other is kept at an inferior and contemptible distance – as may happen in the worst examples of institutional care. The issue then is one of guilt or rather of the potential guilt. The defensive dynamic has to do with protecting ourselves from being in a position of responsibility where the disabled are seen as having been failed. This has to do with protecting the 'inner world' of those who take up roles in relation to the disabled. It has been necessary to look at the unconscious influence of guilt, envy, and reparation in the determination of attitudes as they become expressed in caring roles.

The Distribution and Redistribution of Attitudes

We have argued that roles in relation to disabled people affect the bias of the selection we make from our attitudinal set. Within the roles we take up there are elements that point us in certain directions.

Attitudes are appropriate or not to the realization of certain objectives. We have seen how people draw on relevant parts of an attitudinal set in order to make sense of their relationships to disabled people, and the disabled do likewise to make sense of their environment. A 'good' attitude is thus an attitude that fits with a certain objective. In residential care, for example, the objective might be to compensate for disability and to achieve as well as possible a normal life for residents. In this context, a 'really normal' attitude emphasizing the wholeness of a personality rather than a broken body, is thought of as good or right. But if this is taken to the extent that the separateness of staff is felt to be threatened, and their authority as carers accountable for the well-being of residents is undermined, then such an attitude may become suspect – the limits of the 'really normal' boundary of the self are examined, and it becomes necessary to draw on a 'not whole' concept as well, to accommodate the constraints that in one time and place are thought to be necessary.

All these statements have to be phrased in subjective terms: we say people feel threatened, not that they are threatened, and constraints are thought to be necessary rather than being expressed as immutable. Our view – reinforced by our experience as researchers in this study – is that this is a vital distinction: we have to acknowledge the partialness of our own understanding of the processes we are caught up in. It is difficult to ask the question: how far am I feeling this because of the role I am in? But the difficulty of the question does not diminish its importance – rather the opposite.

In setting up the community care housing project, those managing the process were free to explore the meaning they were putting on the 'really normal' concept of disabled living, but they were always having to check this against their existing roles in the management of a different kind of care: crudely, they had the job of finding 'copers' out of a 'non-coper' system

119

of care, and at the same time providing conditions for meeting the non-coping needs of the copers. It sounds complex and it is: only by examining their roles in relation to the disabled could they attempt such a task. In this example, the examination of roles was not made explicit: the process might have been more easily assimilated if those involved had been able to work more at their own shifting perceptions of their task. But it is a hard thing to ask. As it was – and this must be true generally in such a situation – they found that they were working from inappropriate models and having to adapt to different circumstances with a certain unease and sense of the unknown.

Our work in other settings contributed further to our understanding of the difficulties of a changing perception of task. The marital relationship is at best a mutual caring relationship, where two people are equal but different: if one is then disabled, the difference is made more complex, and the equality becomes suspect. Even where the relationship is less ideal, each individual has an understanding of the relationship, which is disrupted when one becomes physically dependent. Within the family the disabled member may lose his personal autonomy, in a similar way to those in residential care, and, also similarly, other members of the family come to be accountable for his welfare. Within the family system of care, the changing roles, for example wife to nurse, husband to patient, may mean that the wife begins to think according to her idea of a nurse – it is not safe for him to go out; he stays in bed of a morning, so she can clean up – and the husband accepts his diminished role, except perhaps (like a patient) for the occasional outbursts of protest. When both partners are disabled, there is not the same problem. At home they are able to set their own criteria of normality.

The local authority holiday for the disabled was organized from a voluntary organization, but with funding and administrative help from the Social Services Department. Those going on holiday were clients of the social services, and many of the organizers and helpers on the holiday were directly or indirectly accountable to that department. Again this had implications for the way in which the disabled were expected to behave, as clients confirming the goodwill and effectiveness of the system. The clients themselves never forgot their continuing dependence on the social services over the remaining fifty-one weeks in the year. The psychological dependence of the clients was unaffected by this one-week holiday.

THE DEPENDENCY CULTURE AND THE NEGOTIATION OF ALTERNATIVES

That the relationship of the disabled to the able-bodied may be maturely interdependent is theoretically possible. The pressures to keep the disabled in infantile dependence are, however, pervasive, as Gosling has argued in the case of mental disability, and relate to wider societal values, which ambivalently honour the exceptional and reward the conformist (Gosling 1980).

In a dependent role one knows where one is: interdependence necessitates a continuous negotiation between individuals and groups, who are potentially in conflict but pursuing mutual interest. To be dependent has obvious advantages for the displaced and needy in society. To keep them dependent has less obvious but real enough advantages for those who thus retain a controlling influence over what is normal. It would be surprising if the weak and the strong did not enter into a collusive partnership to ensure that they remain weak and strong. The inequality of the relationship furthermore serves to confirm a model of care derived from infantile experience.

Disabled people are useful in provoking others into a caring role; the trouble is that in a dependency culture altruism – giving to others – may be covering up an underlying contempt for those on the receiving end. Likewise, if the dependants are always having to feel grateful, they may have other unexpressed feelings of envy and even hate for those who seem to keep them in a subservient position. A dependency culture, while it is apparently comfortable and stable, thus has its drawbacks. Those who are on the receiving end have to dissemble, obscuring any sense of wholeness they may have in order to present themselves as altogether damaged. A disabled person who has to take on a patient role although he is not ill, for example when his home is a long-stay hospital or hostel staffed by nurses and supervised by doctors, is easily identified by his damaged bit and not by all the rest of him, which is quite sound. So it can happen that adults of sound mind have their lives decided for them. Also it may be uncomfortable for the able-bodied to be the agents of a dependency culture – though this discomfort is more obviously felt when the individual first encounters disabled people, and it wears off in time.

The dependency relationship should imply change, and change for the better: the parent-child relationship has as its desired outcome that the child will grow into a mature adult; the parent is the model of what the child may aspire to become; the patient accepts his dependency on the doctor in the assumption that the doctor is going to get him well – the omnipotence of the doctor is preferred to the anxiety about one's own ability to cope. So a dependency culture has the advantage for the able-bodied that it works as if the disabled are getting better – the inappropriateness of the model is left unexamined.

The urgency of taking up a negotiating position is, however, likely to be felt strongly, or more so, by the disabled themselves. A negotiating position is by definition open-ended: what is appropriate or not is subject to continuous examination and modification.

These elements may help to explain the feeling that we are responsible. It is a way of keeping hold of our sense of control, when we are subject to powerful if unacknowledged feelings of guilt and envy. This constrains attempts at independence. The integration of the disabled, where this is achieved, is usually an integration into membership of more mixed disadvantaged groups, including the mentally handicapped, the elderly, maladjusted young people, and so on. Moving into a different social network, getting a different identity, are thus linked, creating a kind of segregation with its own containing boundaries. As a society, we seem to accept a partial and reluctant responsibility for those who cannot cope with our stressful frenetic model of social interaction and we set up alternative social structures to cope with their dependent needs – and to give us employment, so as to support our continuing frenetic activity.

Real integration – the irrelevance of difference – is rarely achieved, even in family care or open employment. Often 'lucky' ones are happy to work as telephonists or packers, to live outside of institutions and to be useful – but not to realize their true potential. From being third-class citizens they have become second-class citizens.

Those that want to live in their own homes and go out to work that is satisfying to them are likely to be told that they are being unrealistic. A few break through this barrier, but their success does not affect the assumed status of the disabled in society. These individuals are given honorary normal status — an illogical and unstable defensive compromise to cope with the exception without changing the rule. The disabled themselves look for this normal status, claiming that they do not think of themselves as 'disabled'. It is useful to distinguish between 'normal' and 'ordinary' (Bott 1957). They might achieve an 'honorary normal' status, but never become ordinary – part of the assumed social order. 'Honorary normal' is in fact quite extra-ordinary.

But the disabled individual in relation to the group is often anxious to reinforce his membership of the group, even at the expense of his individualism. The fact of disability compounds the anxiety that anyone may feel in relation to the group, and so the disabled individual assesses himself and is assessed in terms of his acceptability in social systems. His individualism is useful for achieving this acceptability, and not something in its own right. If he has an attractive personality, this makes him more acceptable as a disabled person. The disabled are not expected to set norms for the able-bodied. The subsuming of the individual within the group is a throw-back to the kind of social relations that existed when the status of individuals in society was assumed to be fixed and static. The individual is accommodated within the group, but is assumed not to have an impact for change on group life.

For the disabled individual this provides some comfort but not enough. He is thought to be 'courageous' or well adjusted when he puts others at their ease or gives them a warm feeling. But his individualism is threatened in having to make this effort to please. A way round this is to identify with a group that is itself disabled. This is what we mean by the disabled identity. So it is claimed that no one understands the disabled but the disabled themselves. They are their own people and different from others. Even so the disabled are never left on their own. No group has yet existed for which someone has not come along to represent its interests. There is a cost to any kind of social security.

Those who work and live with the disabled have difficulty because they are having to relate both to the individual and the undifferentiated member of the (assumed) group. And this, as it happens, is a characteristic of prejudice. A generalized attitude towards a category of people, black or poor or disabled, is applied indiscriminately to individuals in that category. Sometimes we can also relate to the individual – 'Some of my best friends are black' – but in the background there is always their other group identification, as black or poor or disabled.

The individual is at the same time his own person and the member of an identifiable set or category – a fantasied group membership. We have a relationship with the individual, and feel about him according to how we think he fits with our understanding of his group identity. The group identity that we are foisting on the individual is a loose amalgam of half-formed ideas, and yet we are asking him how he stands in relation to these ideas.

This is the politics of identity. For, in fact, we put up a number of group membership cards, like filters through which we see the individual – though we may have to push him around a bit to get him in focus. We each have our own set of cards. Rather than try to analyse what group membership means to us – for it will be different in every case – it may be more useful to describe how negotiations on the boundary of self (disabled) and environment (handicapping) are affected by the influence of this filter of supposed group identity, through which the individual is forced to peer and wave vigorously if he wants to be recognized as himself.

CONSTRUCTS AND THE DISTRIBUTION OF ATTITUDES

Transactions across the boundary are always problematic. In important respects the parties are divided by the differences; in other equally important respects they are the same – with the shared predicaments of being human and mortal. The difference, moreover, is one of inequality – of more and less capability, of superior and inferior, with associations of guilt and envy. The transaction is therefore one that is likely to evoke in both parties strong and ambivalent feelings. At the intra-personal level these can be dealt with by processes of splitting and projection: these have been discussed earlier. The range of feelings that might be brought into the transaction is enormous, if not infinite. But for the transaction to be sustained, we have seen that the two parties have to agree on a reciprocally acceptable construct of the relationship, which legitimates overt and covert expression of a specific subset of feelings and edits out the rest.

Most transactions across this boundary are managed through reciprocal acceptance of one or another of a very small number of constructs. These are sometimes explicit, often implicit, socially sanctioned ways of behaving. The construct equips the individual with a way of ordering his conflicting and chaotic feelings, permitting some to be expressed and reinforcing his internal mechanisms through which other feelings are repressed and denied or projected. We have argued that these constructs cannot be sustained in isolation from each other. Because no single construct can encompass the contradictions, each construct expresses only part of the reality; but the part has to be justified as if it were the whole; and in order to do this it is necessary to identify at least one other construct as being *un*real, *un*true, *in*correct, *in*-appropriate.

Reflecting the inequality of power between disabled and able-bodied, most constructs have historically been imposed by the latter on the former. The disabled have been socialized into accepting and believing the constructs that the able-bodied have assigned. Over the last fifteen years in Britain this has been changing: to a greater extent, the constructs are the product of mutual negotiation across the boundary.

In the course of this study, in which we took part in, observed, and heard about a great number of these boundary transactions, we have been able to identify only four basic constructs. Every positive co-operative transaction, whether a brief encounter or a sustained relationship, requires the parties to behave according to the expectations (usually tacit) that

125

belong to one, and only one, of these four. Every transaction that is experienced as negative and conflictual, whether it is across the boundary or, say, between two able-bodied persons in response to 'the disabled', is characterized by the competing presence of polarized constructs.

The two that we have mentioned most frequently are:
(1) 'Less-than-whole-person', and
(2) 'Really normal'.
Each of these terms presents a construct of the disabled person and, by implication, an appropriate position to be taken up by the able-bodied party to the transaction. The polarization of these two constructs is manifest. If we turn then to:
(3) 'Enlightened guardianship',
we have a construct of the position of the able-bodied party. As we shall see presently, the reciprocal position that this construct offers for the disabled party is less precise and may be ambiguous. For the moment, however, we can give it the term 'realistic adjustment'. Finally we come to:
(4) 'Disabled power',
which is a convenient shorthand t depict a construct of the disabled by the disabled as being victims of a handicapping society that is dominated by able-bodied interests and values.

In this section, we will discuss the meanings given for these constructs and also explore the dynamic relatedness between them.

'Less-than-whole-person' is a construct that has universal currency. In many societies – including, until very recently, our own – it has been the predominant, if not the only, available construct, accepted by all as the only appropriate basis for the boundary transactions. Usually this has involved the assumption by the able-bodied of obligation, and the reciprocal acknowledgement by the disabled of their inferior and supplicant position. Given the high rate of infant mortality – sometimes induced mortality[1] – the proportion of surviving

---

[1] Exposure of deformed or sickly newborn infants has been widely practised. In our own society, parents and kin of such infants can safely reject such customs as barbarous; they delegate it to the doctors. The criteria vary between individual doctors and also over time: the current adolescent bulge in the spina bifida population, for example, is a consequence of unfounded optimism of doctors in the early 1960s about developments in the medical treatment of this affliction.

cripples in these societies tended not to be burdensome for the rest of the community.

However, in a number of primitive and less primitive societies an opposing construct has also been available: we can call it the 'supernatural' – not less than whole, but with powers above and beyond the ordinary. It is plausible to postulate that this construct would be especially likely to occur in societies practising exposure: to survive one must be very special; and the awe would be a product of guilt. Unfortunately, the search of the anthropological literature that would be needed to test this proposition has been beyond the scope of this study.

Our own society has perhaps had its equivalent of the supernatural construct in the occasional heroic figure, who rises so far above the limitations of his or her disability that the able-bodied majority are left feeling inferior. Douglas Bader was one example; Helen Keller another. What is important is that these have been adopted as heroes by the able-bodied, and not, or not only, by the disabled. Moreover, the criteria for heroic status are set at a remarkably high level. Consequently, the extreme rarity of the heroes could be used as a justification for assigning the 'less-than-whole-person' construct to the mass of the disabled.

'Less-than-whole', though under increasing attack, is still pervasive. It is a construct that enshrines difference and denies sameness. It is manifested in the 'warehousing model' of residential care. The disabled person's physical dependence on others for certain aspects of function is transmuted into a notion of total dependence: that is the only mode in which transactions with the able-bodied are permissible. This allows the able-bodied carers to project onto their charges their own feelings of weakness, inadequacy, impotence, and dependency. With their own superiority safely established, the carers are free to care. Very often then, provided that the patients accept the projections put upon them – if they accept being either infantilized or made into objects – the care is beyond criticism. It has been observed that 'cabbages' are the favourite patients. But there is an alternative pattern, in which the projected weakness and inadequacy are to be punished and expunged. Although it is difficult to pin down specific cases, the circumstantial evidence of sadism is considerable. Fear of sadistic staff is certainly prevalent among those inmates who do not accept the dependent role assigned to them by the 'less-than-whole-person' construct. Also, as we noticed in *A Life Apart*, aids that might reduce handicap are few and far between in institutions governed by this construct: in this way, difference, inferiority, and dependence are confirmed.

A Life Apart described life in total institutions. This life could be in many respects stable and secure, but it was also seen as a social death. The warehousing institution perpetuates the pattern of a stable society, in which roles and status are fixed: the inmates have only one role and their status is unequivocally inferior. In relation to the different and turbulent society outside this is increasingly an anachronism. Total institutions are effective in managing their boundaries so as to keep out this turbulence and suppress individualism within. They have to be, in order to survive: when individualism becomes rampant, the institution is forced to change.

Impetus for change could come at first only from the most privileged of the unfranchised class in the stable society of residential care – from those residents who were most able to think for themselves. *A Life Apart* gave an account of this movement in one residential establishment in the early 1960s. This occurred at a time when, although there was little attention to the plight of the physically disabled, the public conscience was beginning to be pricked by stories of scandalous maltreatment in long-stay hospitals for mental illness and subnormality.

The 'really-normal' construct emerged therefore as a liberal protest, by both disabled and able-bodied, against the totalitarian approach. It was a rejection of 'less-than-whole' – and also by implication of the 'heroic' model. For in the 'less-than-whole', and also in the 'heroic', difference is emphasized, and sameness – shared humanity – is behaviourally, if not verbally, denied. In 'really normal' – identified in *A Life Apart* with the 'horticultural model' – it is the reverse: energy is devoted to denial of difference and dependency. The goal is independence, which may be seen as attainable through treatment, prosthetics, slave-labour, or even sheer will-power.

By implication, independence is regarded as the normal state of the able-bodied and once the disabled have attained it the problematic boundary will vanish. In this sense, 'really-normal' may be a misleading term: it implies absence of handicap. What we are concerned to emphasize is the element of denial, which is often associated with idealization – for example, of the courage of the disabled person in coping with the handicap. To this extent the 'heroic' is incorporated in the 'really normal'. The able-bodied party to the transaction can paradoxically come to feel that not being disabled is itself a handicap. This makes for a sense of egalitarianism in transactions across the boundary, which is satisfying to both parties; and their relationship is sustained by their joint rejection of the 'less-than-whole-person' construct.

We saw examples of the polarization of these two constructs and the tension between them in Chapter 2. The notion of normal life in the community invariably evoked all the caveats from those involved in residential care, who were then identified with 'less-than-whole-person', against which 'really-normal' had to be re-asserted. Both parties in these transactions were dedicated to the interests of this set of disabled people who would be moving out of residential establishments into 'the community'; yet they often seemed to be operating from polarized positions.

It was argued in *A Life Apart* that both these constructs were inadequate. 'Less-than-whole-person', incorporated in the warehousing model, recognized the physical dependency, expanded this into total dependency, and made no room for individuals' wishes, needs, and capabilities to be autonomous. 'Really-normal', on the other hand, the construct of the horticultural model, was attractive in its assertion of individual autonomy and capacity for development, but tended to deny and perhaps to denigrate inescapable needs for dependency, physical and psychological. We proposed in that book a model of residential care that explicitly provided for both sets of needs – the dependent and the independent. 'Enlightened guardianship' is the construct implied in that model. It seems to have emerged in the last ten years.

Occupying what in political terms might be the 'social democrat' position, it draws adherents from both 'less-than-whole-person' and 'really-normal'. If we use a family analogy, it corresponds perhaps to the relationship between parents and adolescent offspring. It moves away from the infantilization of 'less-than-whole-person' but clings to the notion of responsibility; it acknowledges the drives towards autonomy and independence, but at the same time asks of disabled people that they should be realistic about their aims and aspirations.

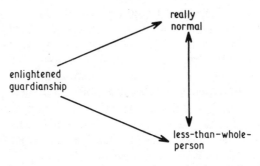

(The arrowhead ➤ represents 'not-me' or 'not-us')

Within 'enlightened guardianship', therefore, adjustment to reality is an important ideology. But both 'adjustment' and 'reality' are elusive concepts, especially since the disabled are asked to accept a picture of reality and a process of adjustment to it that are defined by the able-bodied. And confusion is worse confounded in that 'adjustment' – with perhaps more controlling and coercive overtones – is also advanced as an ideology by proponents of 'less-than-whole-person'. Hence transactions within the 'enlightened guardianship' construct have an unpredictable, or at best oscillating character – which of course is consistent with adolescence. But whereas adolescence is – usually – transient, this is a permanent state, in which the battles over dependence and autonomy can be fought and re-fought over and over again. 'Enlightened guardianship' therefore has the unenviable task of struggling to hold to a centralist position in an essentially polarized world; and, as the above diagram shows, it depends for its definition on the existence of that polarized world.

Both 'less-than-whole-person' and 'enlightened guardianship' are constructs imposed or proposed by the able-bodied majority. 'Really normal' obviously implies that the able-bodied are the reference group for normality. But it is a construct that disabled people themselves have also espoused in protest against imposition of 'less-than-whole-person'.

The two stages of development of a minority group seeking recognition in society are characterized in the first place by a desire to please and secondly by a need to assert one's individuality. In race we can see the progression from Uncle Tom-ism to Black Power. Homosexuality is now less a discreet aberration tolerated by a liberal society and more an overt expression of positive difference – as people 'come out' and even march under a Gay Lib banner. The women's movement displays a new assertiveness about femaleness, for example in the proposition that 'when God created man She was only joking'. This shows a determination that it is essentially normal – all right and certainly not subservient – to be different both from the male stereotype and the stereotypic male view of women.

In the same way that traditionally the well-adjusted woman was seen to be rather good at fitting into a man's world, so to be disabled and 'well adjusted' also traditionally has required a certain tact, a sensitiveness to one's place in the world, or – put another way – a willingness to accept uncritically the projective assumptions of the normal able-bodied that the disabled may be weak and inferior but they are lovable and capable of being cared for.

The 'really normal' construct was therefore a staging post in the 'coming out' of the disabled. It was a picture of reality that they were imposing on the able-bodied majority. But to the extent that it could also be adopted by the 'liberal' able-bodied it was not wholly satisfactory to the disabled. Hence the last decade, in parallel with 'enlightened guardianship', has seen the emergence of a small but vocal minority asserting what we call here 'disabled power'.

The disabled-power argument runs something like this: 'I am a whole human being and as such have the same legitimate rights as all others, whether disabled or not. It is society that is handicapping me by depriving me of these rights.' Hence it is oppositional to all three of the other constructs.

It is threatening to the traditional 'less-than-whole-person'

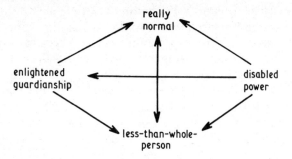

position because it shifts the discourse from the language of privilege to the language of rights. It rejects the social democrat position of 'enlightened guardianship' as imposing the dominant able-bodied values on a disabled world. And it is most threatening of all to the liberal adherents of 'really normal', because it is a product exclusively of the disabled themselves, who cast all able-bodied in the role of enemies and reject them as allies. (In this it corresponds closely to the Black Power and Women's Liberation movements: it unmasks the patronizing element lurking behind the egalitarianism.) Difference is not something to be ashamed of or denied, but to assert, as with 'Black is beautiful'. And if white liberals begin to concur with 'Black is beautiful', then the blackness – that which is different – has to be asserted by a minority in more extreme and outrageous ways, which will alienate all whites.

To survive, therefore, the 'disabled power' construct needs the able-bodied constructs as negative reference points. For this reason it can rarely mediate specific relationships between able-bodied and disabled people – except in confrontation. Yet its existence as an ideology has effects. To the extent that it captures the 'really normal' position, with all its positive connotations, the displaced able-bodied liberals are pushed into 'enlightened guardianship'. Precluded from identifying with the disabled the liberals resort to trying to be understanding. And 'enlightened guardianship' itself becomes less assertively positive and less distinguishable from 'less-than-whole-person'.

One can see this process occurring in quite simple transactions. For example, in a seminar that included both able-bodied and disabled participants, one speaker could be seen as a clear protagonist of 'enlightened guardianship'. Then one of the disabled men began to speak of rights and demands. The speaker immediately and visibly shifted to a counter-attack from the 'less-than-whole-person' position. The process may be depicted like this.

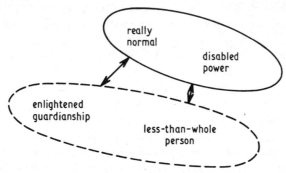

The constructs identified here all involve some splitting and projection. To some extent they are interdependent. Thus the 'less-than-whole-person' construct offers a convenient not-us to a relationship sustained by the 'really-normal' value. From any one stance, the others can be dismissed as 'unrealistic'.

Therefore the reciprocal 'not-us' set provided by these constructs goes some way towards dealing with the problem of the inter-personal relationship between able-bodied and disabled: some of the discomfort is, in fact, projected outside. The reciprocity is not total, in that the existence of other constructs can be seen as a threat rather than a support to the 'less-than-whole-person' position. However, staff in an institution operating on that construct (or parents of a handicapped child) have less need to mobilize a not-us in alliance with those in their care: they themselves have adequate power to control the boundary and define the position of their disabled dependants within it.

THE REDISTRIBUTION OF ATTITUDES

Our proposition is that the great majority of able-bodied/disabled transactions are mediated through one or other of these four constructs. However, there may be a residual category of people – including ourselves? – who are dissatisfied with these and seeking another position. The problem is that such a search implies the existence of a spectrum, whereas our analysis indicates that what we are dealing with is polarization and ambivalence. The wished-for relationship combines two dualities: it should be 'normal' and it should be 'realistic'. At the moment these are incompatible.

Meanwhile, the distribution of attitudes around the disabled has as its function the monitoring and social control of what disabled people are allowed to do. The boundaries of what is allowable may evidently be changed, expanded, or contracted as there are pressures to confine them to a sick role in society – and also to recognize a common humanity, as physical normality is seen not to be essential to a citizen role. Toleration of difference – as in matters of race or sexual politics – requires the re-examination of stereotypes projected on to others. We have seen in this study that even benign projections have their problems, demanding of the disabled that they act out a successful integration of others' own sense of damage. Any shift in the status of disabled people is achieved only by negotiation, whereby the criteria of their acceptability by the able-bodied are revised. But attitudes are not fixed entities: in this study our experience has been that instead of a drawing on conflicting and contrasted standpoints, as the disabled relate to others in different roles, there has been an allowing for more or less dependency and independence. For the able-bodied, the opposite end of the continuum from caring may feel like impotence, and from protectiveness – indifference. The question remains: how much are disabled people made to feel inferior or have their autonomy undermined in order that others may feel better about them? This is a challenge also for those who are disabled, for they have to balance the social costs of their dependency – and being looked after does arouse the envy of others – with the advantages of which some have little experience, of living as whole people in damaged bodies.

The challenge in looking at the redistribution of attitudes has implications in three major ways.

(1) The modification of professional perspectives

Differences of role between professional carers – for example, between doctors, nurses, para-medicals, social workers – are readily exploited for the purpose of containing ambivalence towards disability. The specific skills of each discipline allow the protagonists to claim a special relationship towards disabled people and so to act out with each other the problems of meeting the physical dependency needs of their clients or patients, while at the same time acknowledging their personal autonomy as citizens. At the worst, the protagonists can argue among themselves; while, between them, they are colluding to keep the disabled people in an uncertain and unstable confusion about their social skills. (A social worker selection board appoints a disabled applicant as clerical officer, and a medical officer bars the appointment. Or one may think how agencies see their task as compensating for the ill-effects of other agencies.)

We suggest that, both in their training and practice, it would be useful for those taking caring roles in relation to disabled people to explore for themselves how they are interdependent with others in maintaining a distribution of attitudes according to the different constructs that we have outlined. Those who see defects in the 'medical model' may also have to examine the limitations of, say, a social work model, and vice versa. We do not underestimate the difficulties of this exercise: it recognizes the acceptance of contradictions in one's own position, and the re-integration of aspects of the relationship, that may otherwise be discerned and attacked in others. Our hope is that this account of our own exploration of these issues will act both as a stimulus and an aid to a continuing re-appraisal of the realities of the boundaries of us/not-us in the care relationship.

(2) Disabled action

This study also demonstrates that disabled people themselves are not passive participants in the processes of discrimination, positive or negative, to which they are subjected. On the one hand there is the possibility of collusion with able-bodied attempts to maintain them in an undynamic dependency relationship. But also there may be a compensating rejection of the common areas of concern, so that disabled people can only struggle in what they see as an alien environment. They may choose to negotiate from a 'really normal' or 'disabled power' standpoint, or even feel most comfortable in a dependency culture, to which they have become accustomed – but the opportunity to change their status may further involve the challenge – similar to that facing the carers – to work at the contradictions of their own position. To deny altogether their disability can only encourage others more determinedly to see them as not quite whole, and yet if they accept without protest the projections of the able-bodied they in effect abnegate their own autonomy. In a redistribution of attitudes they have the hope of acceptance both as physically dependent and as normally autonomous in their psychological and social status.

(3) Legislation and financial provision

The study has demonstrated how statutory provision for disabled people may serve to confirm some attitudes and constrain the expression of others. Legislation lays down definitions of disability and makes distinctions within disability by mixed and inconsistent criteria: is it the cause of the disability that counts, or is it the consequences? It reinforces a dependency culture while providing some resources to promote independence. (Community housing was still subject to legislation to do with residential care. Disabled people become experts on 'welfare' provision.) Economic constraints ensure that we maintain distinctions and differences that are psychologically confusing and inconsistent.

As a redistribution of attitudes gives greater emphasis to 'disabled power', economic 'reality' is seen as retaining a 'not whole' status for disabled people. Our view is that the conflict between the different constructs will become increasingly overt, as disabled people make demands in their own right that they have much greater control over the economic and welfare resources made available to them, so that they become consumers and indeed buyers rather than clients of the services that they need. Only then would they influence and choose for themselves the quality of life available to them with the same freedom as the able-bodied.

136

References

Allport, G. W. (1935) Attitudes. In C. Murchison (ed.) *Handbook of Social Psychology*. Worcester: Clark University Press.

Bannister, D. (ed.) (1977) *New Perspectives in Personal Construct Theory*. London: Academic Press.

Bannister, D. and Mair, J. M. M. (1968) *The Evaluation of Personal Constructs*. London: Academic Press.

Bolderson, H. (1980) The origins of the disabled persons employment quota and its symbolic significance. *Journal of Social Policy* **9** (2): 169–86.

Bolt, R. (1972) Organizations that serve social values. In J. M. Thomas and W. G. Bennis (eds) *Management of Change and Conflict*. Harmondsworth: Penguin.

Bott, E. (1957) *Family and Social Networks*. London: Tavistock Publications.

Brattgard, S. O. (1974) Social and psychological aspects of the situation of the disabled. In D. M. Boswell and J. M. Wingrove (eds) *The Handicapped Person in the Community*. London: Tavistock Publications and Open University Press.

Committee On Restrictions Against Disabled People (CORAD) (1979) *Discrimination Against Disabled People – Invitation to Comment*. London.

Dartington, T. (1971) *Task Force*. London: Mitchell Beazley.

Dartington, T. (1979) Fragmentation and integration in health care: the referral process and social brokerage. *Sociology of Health and Illness* **1**: 12–39.

Dartington, T. (1980) *Family Care of Old People*. London: Souvenir Press.

Dartington, T. and Miller, E. J. (1977) A brave face for the handicapped. *Social Work Today* **9** (11): 9–10.

Davis, F. (1961) Deviance disavowal: the management of strained interaction by the physically handicapped. *Social Problems* **9** (2): 120–32.

Disability Alliance (1980) *Disability Rights Handbook for 1980*. London.

Elliot, J. (1975) *Living in Hospital*. The social needs of people in long-term care, with checklist of 100 questions. London: Kings Fund.

Fransella, F. and Bannister, D. (1977) *A Manual for Repertory Grid Techniques*. London: Academic Press.

Goffman, E. (1963) *Stigma: notes on the management of a spoiled identity*. Harmondsworth: Penguin.

Gosling, R. (1980) The role of the Richmond Fellowship in the field of welfare. *The Richmond Fellowship's Report, 1979–80*: 23–31.

Halloran, J. D. (1967) *Attitude Formation and Change*. Leicester: Leicester University Press.

Hofling, C. K., Brotzman, E., Dalrymple, S., Graves, N., and Pierce, C. N. (1966) An experimental study in nurse-physician relationships. *Journal of Nervous and Mental Disease* **143** (2): 171–80.

A Life Together

Hunt, P. (ed.) (1966) *Stigma: the experience of disability*. London: Geoffrey Chapman.

Hunt, P. (1972) Parasite people. (Review of *A Life Apart*.) *Cheshire Smile* (magazine of the Cheshire Foundation), Autumn: 15–18.

Illich, I. (1974) *Medical Nemesis*. London: Calder & Boyars.

Janowitz, M. (1966) Foreword. In D. Street, R. D. Vinter, and C. Perrow, *Organization for Treatment: a comparative study of institutions for delinquents*. New York: The Free Press; London: Collier-Macmillan.

Jansen, E. (ed.) (1980) *The Therapeutic Community: outside the hospital*. London: Croom Helm.

Katz, D. (1960) The irrational approach to the study of attitudes. *Public Opinion Quarterly* **24**: 163–204.

Kelly, G. A. (1955) *The Psychology of Personal Constructs*. 2 vols. New York: Norton.

Klein, M. and Riviere, J. (1937) *Love, Hate and Reparation*. London: Hogarth Press.

Krugman, H. E. (1965) The impact of television advertising. Learning without involvement. *Public Opinion Quarterly* **XXIX** (3): 349–56.

Kushlick, A. (1975) Some ways of setting, monitoring and attaining objectives for services for disabled people. *Research Report, No. 116*. Health Care Evaluation Research Team, Wessex Regional Health Authority.

Marris, P. (1974) *Loss and Change*. London: Routledge & Kegan Paul.

Menzies, I. E. P. (1960) A case-study in the functioning of social systems as a defence against anxiety. *Human Relations* **13**: 95–121. Reprinted (1970) by Tavistock Institute of Human Relations, London.

Miller, E. J. (1975) Demands and problems of face-to-face work with people. In an Open University post-experience course, 'The Handicapped Person in the Community', Units 1–10, Block 3, Part I, *Providing Supportive Services*. Milton Keynes: Open University Press.

— (1977) Organizational development and industrial democracy: a current case-study. In C. Cooper (ed.) *Organizational Development in the UK and USA: a joint education*. London: Macmillan.

— (1979) Autonomy, dependency and organizational change. In D. Towell and C. Harries (eds) *Innovation in Patient Care: an action research study of change in a psychiatric hospital*. London: Croom Helm.

Miller, E. J. and Gwynne, G. V. (1972) *A Life Apart: a pilot study of residential institutions for the physically handicapped and young chronic sick*. London: Tavistock Publications.

— (1973) Dependence, independence, and counter-dependence in residential institutions for incurables. In R. Gosling (ed.), *Support, Innovation, and Autonomy*. London: Tavistock Publications.

Miller, E. J. and Rice, A. K. (1967) *Systems of Organization*. London: Tavistock Publications.

National Council of Social Service (1967) *Caring for People: staffing residential homes*. London: Allen & Unwin.

Oliver, M. (1978) Disability, adjustment and family life – some theoretical considerations. Paper at conference, Spinal Injuries Association.

References

PHAB (1977) *Introducing PHAB* (leaflet). London.

Report of the Royal Commission on the Law relating to Mental Illness and Mental Deficiency (1957) Cmd 169. London: HMSO.

Scott, R. A. (1974) The construction of conception of stigma by professional experts. In Boswell, D. M. and Wingrove, J. M. (eds), *The Handicapped Person in the Community*. London: Tavistock Publications.

Simkins, J. and Tichner, V. (1978) *Whose Benefit?* London: The Economist Intelligence Unit and Disability Alliance.

Snowdon (1976) *Integrating the Disabled*. Working Party Report, National Fund for Research into Crippling Diseases.

Stevens, R. (1975) Attitudes. In an Open University Social Sciences foundation course, 'Making Sense of Society', Block 7, *Attitudes and Beliefs*. Milton Keynes: Open University Press.

Storr, A. (1970) *Integrity of the Personality*. Harmondsworth: Penguin.

Topliss, E. (1979) *Provision for the Disabled*. Oxford: Blackwell.

Towell, D. (1979) A 'social systems' approach to research and to change in nursing care. *International Journal of Nursing Studies* **16**: 111–21.

Towell, D. and Dartington, T. (1976) Encouraging innovations in hospital care. *Journal of Advanced Nursing* **1**: 391–98.

Towell, D. and Harries, C. (eds) (1979) *Innovation in Patient Care: an action research study of change in a psychiatric hospital*. London: Croom Helm.

Woman's Realm (1978), 25 February.

Woods, D. (1978) *Biko*. London: Paddington Press.

Wright, B. (1960) *Physical Disability: a psychological approach*. New York: Harper.

Younghusband, E. (1978) *Social Work in Britain: 1950–1975. A follow-up study.* 2 vols. London: Allen & Unwin.

Name Index

Subject Index

143